GOTHAM CENTRAL

BOOK THREE: ON THE FREAK BEAT

GOTHAM CENTRAL

BOOK THREE: ON THE FREAK BEAT

Written by
GREG RUCKA & ED BRUBAKER

Pencils by
MICHAEL LARK
STEFANO GAUDIANO
JASON ALEXANDER

Inks by
STEFANO GAUDIANO
JASON ALEXANDER
KANO
GARY AMARO

Batman created
by BOB KANE

Colors by
LEE LOUGHRIDGE

Letters by
CLEM ROBINS

Covers by
MICHAEL LARK (#23-30)
and
CLIFF CHIANG (#31)

**DETECTIVE
JOELY BARTLETT**
Partner of Vincent
Del Arrazio.

**CAPTAIN
MAGGIE SAWYER**
First shift commander;
formerly head of Metropolis
Special Crimes Unit.

**SGT. VINCENT
DEL ARRAZIO**
First shift
second-in-command;
partner of Joely Bartlett.

**DETECTIVE
CRISPUS ALLEN**
Partner of Renee Montoya.

GOTHAM CITY
POLICE DEPARTMENT
MAJOR CRIMES UNIT

LT. DAVID CORNWELL
Second shift commander.

**SGT. JACKSON
"SARGE" DAVIES**
Second shift
co-second-in-command;
partner of Crowe.

SECOND
SHIFT

**DETECTIVE
JOSH AZEVEDA**
Partner of Trey Hartley.

DETECTIVE CROWE
Partner of Sarge Davies.

**DETECTIVE
NATE PATTON**
Partner of Romy Chandler.

**DETECTIVE
TREY HARTLEY**
Partner of Josh Azeveda.

**DETECTIVE
MARCUS DRIVER**
Last MCU officer to be selected
by former Commissioner James
W. Gordon.

LT. RON PROBSON
Second shift
co-second-in-command.

**DETECTIVE
ERIC COHEN**
Partner of Andi Kasinsky.

**DETECTIVE
ANDI KASINSKY**
Partner of Eric Cohen.

**DETECTIVE 2ND GRADE
RENEE MONTOYA**
Partner of Crispus Allen.

**DETECTIVE
TOMMY BURKE**
Partner of
Dagmar Procjnow.

**DETECTIVE
DAGMAR
PROCJNOW**
Partner of Tommy Burke.

**DETECTIVE
JOSEPHINE "JOSIE
MAC" MACDONALD**
Has the distinction of being
the first MCU officer selected after
Jim Gordon's retirement.

**DETECTIVE
ROMY CHANDLER**
Partner of Nate Patton.

POLICE
SUPPORT

NORA FIELDS
City coroner.

STACY
Receptionist;
only person permitted to
operate the Bat-Signal.

**COMMISSIONER
MICHAEL AKINS**
Former commissioner
for Gateway City,
replaced James W. Gordon.

JIM CORRIGAN
GCPD crime scene
investigator.

JAMES W. GORDON
Former Gotham City police
commissioner, and 20-year
veteran of the force. Currently
teaches criminology at
Gotham University.

MATT IDELSON   EDITOR-ORIGINAL SERIES
NACHIE CASTRO   ASSISTANT EDITOR-ORIGINAL SERIES
ANTON KAWASAKI   EDITOR
ROBBIN BROSTERMAN   DESIGN DIRECTOR – BOOKS
BRAINCHILD STUDIOS/NYC   PUBLICATION DESIGN

BOB HARRAS   SENIOR VP – EDITOR-IN-CHIEF, DC COMICS

DIANE NELSON   PRESIDENT
DAN DIDIO AND JIM LEE   CO-PUBLISHERS
GEOFF JOHNS   CHIEF CREATIVE OFFICER
AMIT DESAI   SENIOR VP – MARKETING & FRANCHISE MANAGEMENT
AMY GENKINS   SENIOR VP – BUSINESS & LEGAL AFFAIRS
NAIRI GARDINER   SENIOR VP – FINANCE
JEFF BOISON   VP – PUBLISHING PLANNING
MARK CHIARELLO   VP – ART DIRECTION & DESIGN
JOHN CUNNINGHAM   VP – MARKETING
TERRI CUNNINGHAM   VP – EDITORIAL ADMINISTRATION
LARRY GANEM   VP – TALENT RELATIONS & SERVICES
ALISON GILL   SENIOR VP – MANUFACTURING & OPERATIONS
HANK KANALZ   SENIOR VP – VERTIGO & INTEGRATED PUBLISHING
JAY KOGAN   VP – BUSINESS & LEGAL AFFAIRS, PUBLISHING
JACK MAHAN   VP – BUSINESS AFFAIRS, TALENT
NICK NAPOLITANO   VP – MANUFACTURING ADMINISTRATION
SUE POHJA   VP – BOOK SALES
FRED RUIZ   VP – MANUFACTURING OPERATIONS
COURTNEY SIMMONS   SENIOR VP – PUBLICITY
BOB WAYNE   SENIOR VP – SALES

Cover by Cliff Chiang.

DC Comics, 1700 Broadway, New York, NY 10019
A Warner Bros. Entertainment Company
Printed by Transcontinental Interglobe, Beauceville, QC, Canada. 10/10/14. Fourth Printing.
ISBN: 978-1-4012-3232-0

Library of Congress Cataloging-in-Publication Data

Rucka, Greg.
   Gotham central. Book three, On the freak beat / Greg Rucka, Ed Brubaker, Michael Lark,
Stefano Gaudiano.
      p. cm.
   "Originally published in single magazine form in Gotham Central 23-31."
   ISBN 978-1-4012-3232-0
   1. Police—Comic books, strips, etc. 2. Graphic novels. I. Brubaker, Ed. II. Lark, Michael.
III. Gaudiano, Stefano. IV. Title. V. Title: On the freak beat.
   PN6728.G65R835 2012
   741.5'973—dc23
                              2012025236

SUSTAINABLE   Certified Chain of Custody
FORESTRY   Promoting Sustainable Forestry
INITIATIVE   www.sfiprogram.org
SFI-00507
This label only applies to the text section.

CORRIGAN

Written by
GREG RUCKA

Art by
MICHAEL LARK & STEFANO GAUDIANO

Colors by
LEE LOUGHRIDGE

Letters by
CLEM ROBINS

POLICE
DEPARTMENT
OF GOTHAM

Inspector Manuel Esperanza

DOB: 06/09/1959
Eyes: Brown
Rank: Detective
Dept. Internal Affairs

Badge #3585
Height: 6'2"
Weight: 182
Hair Color: Black

HAM CITY
ICE DEPARTMENT

INITIAL REPORT XXX FOLLOW

/14/04 DATE/TIME OF OCCU

S NAME - LAST, FIRST, M.I.

STRUCTION OF OCCURRENCE - SUSPECT NAME/NICKNAME/ALIAS - INCLUDE METHOD OF ENTRY AND ESCAPE - INCLUDE UNIQUE AND U

Previously in Gotham Central:

Detective Crispus Allen and his partner Detective Renee Montoya are considered by many in the M.C.U. to be the strongest partner pair under Captain Maggie Sawyer's command. What started as mutual respect between the two has matured into a genuine friendship that thus far has survived every test Gotham has thrown at them.

But even the best detectives keep secrets from their partners. Last year, Two-Face's long-standing infatuation with Montoya reached crescendo. He attempted to destroy her life, professional and personal, first by outing her as lesbian, and then by framing her for murder. The I.A.D. investigation was lead by Inspector Manny Esperanza, and in the end, Montoya was cleared of all wrong doing. Since then, sh attempted to build a new life both in the M.C.U., and with her lover, Daria "

DARIA HERN

Face Captured After Jail
out and Kidnapping

HARVEY DENT (File Photo)

MONTOYA, RENEE
GOTHAM CIT
JAIL DIV.

6 2 3 6

MONTOYA, RENEE
GOTHAM CITY
JAIL DIV.

9

SUNDAY WILL WORK, BUT IT HAS TO BE AFTER ELEVEN.

DORE AND I WERE THINKING WE'D COME OVER AFTER CHURCH, DARIA CAN *WOW* US WITH HER CULINARY SKILL.

SHE WILL, TOO. SHE DOES A *FRITTATA* LIKE NOBODY'S BUSINESS, TELL YOU THAT MUCH.

YOUR WOMAN CAN *FRITTATA-TA-TA* ALL SHE *LIKES,* BUT I'VE GOT *TWO* KIDS, AND THEY SPEAK *ONE* WORD AT SUNDAY BREAKFAST...

...AND THAT WORD IS *"WAFFLES."*

SHE DOES WAFFLES LIKE NOBODY'S BUSINESS, TOO.

YOU OR ME THIS TIME?

ALL YOURS, PARTNER.

DETECTIVE MONTOYA, YOU *STILL* TRYING TO *PAY* ME FOR YOUR FOOD?

I AM, GINNY.

GIRL, WE GOT *GANGS* SHOOTING THIS CITY TO *HELL* AND *BACK* RIGHT NOW!

I TOLD *YOU* AND I TOLD YOUR *PARTNER,* YOUR MONEY'S NO GOOD HERE.

SHE'S *SLOW,* GINNY, YOU HAVE TO *FORGIVE* HER.

I LEAVE *FORGIVENESS* TO THE ALMIGHTY, DETECTIVE ALLEN.

CORRIGAN PART ONE

YOU *FEEL* THAT? IT'S LIKE WALKING INTO A *SPONGE*.

HALF PAST *MIDNIGHT*, THE HUMIDITY'S *STILL* A ZILLION PERCENT.

PLEASE TELL ME THE *AIR CONDITIONER* WORKS.

OKAY, THE AIR CONDITIONER WORKS.

SMART-ASS

AND SEXY, TOO.

HUNTING PARTY.

B.T.M.

CALL FOR BACKUP.

CENTRAL SIX-CHARLIE-TANGO, TEN THIRTY-ONE, EIGHT THOUSAND BLOCK OF HEWLIS, REQUEST BACKUP.

SIX-CHARLIE-TANGO STAND BY.

SIX-CHARLIE-TANGO, BE ADVISED, BACKUP EN ROUTE...

...E.T.A. *FIVE* MINUTES.

KRAK KRAK KRAK
KRAK KRAK

FIVE MINUTES.

YOU WANT TO **WAIT**?

THAT'S WHAT I THOUGHT.

THEY STARTED WITHOUT US.

HOW RUDE.

JESUS, CRIS, THIS KID'S **SIXTEEN** IF A DAY.

YOU RECOGNIZE THIS **TAG**? IT'S **NOT** BURNLEY TOWN MASSIVE.

KRAK KRAK
KRAK KRAK

CHAK CHAK
CHAK CHAK

HNNN

MUH-MUH-
FUHNNNN

MAN, CAN'T *SEE* HIM!

KEEP LOOKING! HE AROUND HERE SOMEWHERE!

POLICE! *FREEZE!*

LOSE THE GUNS, TOUGH GUY.

BIG FRONT, YOU *SOUND* LIKE A SMALL GIRL.

MY *PISTOL* MAKES UP FOR IT.

NOW *LOSE* THE GUNS, I WON'T SAY IT AGAIN.

SHE MEANS YOU, TOO.

ON THE *FLOOR*, BOTH OF YOU.

WE BEEN *HAD*, BUNK. SPIDER'S DONE *BOUGHT* HIMSELF SOME *POLICE*...

...THEY PROBABLY *WIPE* FOR HIM, TOO.

THE HELL ARE YOU TALKING ABOUT?

HEY, I KNOW MY *RIGHTS*, I DON'T TELL YOU *SQUAT*.

YEAH? THEN *SHUT UP*.

KRK

THERE'S *ONE* MORE.

FIVE-TO-ONE IT'S A *FREAK*.

HOLD UP.

ESPERANZA.

GOT HERE ABOUT FIVE MINUTES AGO, CAPTAIN.

DAMMIT.

DETECTIVE ALLEN!

UP HERE, CAPTAIN.

STOP TALKING TO ESPERANZA.

IF HE'S *NOT* SUPPOSED TO TALK TO ME, HOW AM I SUPPOSED TO *CLEAR* HIM FOR THE *SHOOT?*

YOU COULD GIVE HIM A COUPLE MINUTES TO COLLECT HIMSELF.

YOU KNOW THE *RULES,* MAGGIE. I HAVE TO TAKE THE *STATEMENT* AS SOON AS POSSIBLE.

YOU ALL RIGHT, CRIS?

MY STOMACH'S SETTLING.

HOW'S RENEE?

SHE'S AT THE *HOSPITAL.* TWO OF HER *RIBS* CRACKED, BUT OTHERWISE SHE'S FINE.

THANK GOD FOR THAT.

LET'S FINISH THIS UP, DETECTIVE.

RIGHT...I...WE'D *CUFFED* THE TWO IN THE *APARTMENT,* THEN HEARD SOMETHING IN THE *HALL.*

I WENT TO CIRCLE AROUND, AS I WAS COMING OUT I HEARD THE *SHOTS.* MY WEAPON WAS ALREADY *OUT.*

I CAME AROUND, SAW THE *FREAK.*

"BLACK SPIDER." REAL NAME WAS JOHNNY LAMONICA.

RIGHT, I SAW HIM *HERE,* HE WAS *SHOOTING* INTO THE *APARTMENT.*

HE'D ALREADY HIT DETECTIVE MONTOYA?

IT WAS...IT WAS ALL AT ONCE, HE'D HIT HER, SHE WAS FALLING, HE WAS *STILL* SHOOTING.

THAT MUST HAVE BEEN WHEN HE HIT THE *OTHER* TWO, THE ONES WE'D *ARRESTED.*

THAT'S WHAT I SAW.

HE WAS POINTING A GUN--ONE OF HIS GUNS--AT RENEE, HE LEVELED THE *OTHER* ONE AT ME...

I STARTED *SHOOTING.*

THAT'S IT, THAT'S ALL.

NOTHING YOU WANT TO ADD?

HE SAID THAT'S *ALL,* MANNY.

I'M GONNA NEED THE *STATEMENT* IN *WRITING.* HE CAN DO THAT WHEN HE GETS BACK TO CENTRAL.

YOU'LL HAVE IT.

MONTOYA'S AT GENERAL?

THEY TOOK HER TO ST. LUKE'S, ALONG WITH THE *OTHER* BANGER.

I'LL TALK TO HER *THERE,* THEN.

NEED YOUR *WEAPON,* DETECTIVE.

...RIGHT.

YOU'LL BE GETTING IT BACK, I'M SURE.

LET'S GET YOU BACK TO CENTRAL.

HUH?

YEAH... YEAH, LET'S DO THAT...

JUST FOR THE **STATEMENT,** CRIS, THEN YOU CAN GO HOME.

NO, I'M FINE, CAPTAIN, IT'S OKAY.

RENEE'S OKAY?

SHE'LL BE FINE.

SHE SAYS YOU SAVED HER LIFE.

FINISHED WITH THE **DOORWAY,** YOU WANT TO TAKE SOME SHOTS OUT THERE.

I SWEAR WE'RE GONNA BE HERE UNTIL **NOON,** CORRIGAN.

HEY, IT'S ALL GOOD, FRANKIE.

NOTHING LIKE A NICE BIG **GANG WAR** TO BOOST THE **SAVINGS ACCOUNT...**

...WE GET **O.T.,** AND THE **SKELS** KILL EACH OTHER OFF.

THAT'S **WIN-WIN** WHERE I'M SITTING...

...MONEY IN **POCKET...**

...NO, HER NAME IS MONTOYA, RENEE MONTOYA.

ARE YOU FAMILY?

I'M HER **PARTNER.**

THEN I **NEED** TO SEE A **BADGE.**

NO, I'M **NOT** A COP, I'M HER...WE **LIVE** TOGETHER.

SHE'S YOUR GIRLFRIEND.

SHE'S MY **PARTNER.**

WHATEVER, YOU'RE GOING TO HAVE TO **WAIT** HERE, LIKE EVERYONE ELSE.

CHEF HERNANDEZ.

OH, CHRIST.

I GUESS I MADE AN **IMPRESSION.**

YES, INSPECTOR ESPERANZA, I'D SAY THAT YOU DID, WHAT WITH YOU **USING** ME TO TRY TO GET AT **RENEE.**

I WAS DOING MY JOB, MS. HERNANDEZ.

WON'T LET YOU BACK TO SEE HER?

I'M NOT **FAMILY** ENOUGH.

NOT LIKE **ANY** OF HER FAMILY IS HERE, OF COURSE.

WELL, COME ON.

THIS FROM THE HEWLIS STREET SHOOTING?

YEAH, ONE OF THE B.T.M. LEAD-SLINGERS...

...GOT *WINGED* DURING THE EXCHANGE, I GUESS.

I'M SUPPOSED TO TAKE HIM DOWN TO CENTRAL SOON AS HE'S *RELEASED.*

SEE THAT YOU DO.

HE WAS ABOUT TO PULL THE TRIGGER ON ME, INSPECTOR, SWEAR TO GOD THE *NEXT* BURST WAS COMING FOR MY *HEAD.*

CRIS HADN'T LIT HIM UP, I'D BE DEAD RIGHT NOW.

I DON'T *DOUBT IT.*

WORD WAS THAT THE PENGUIN HAD ARRANGED FOR LAMONICA TO DO SOME WORK FOR THE FIVE FAMILIES.

LOOKS LIKE THE B.T.M. TRIED TO *PREEMPT* THAT BY TAKING HIM OUT, THAT'S WHAT THE TWO OF YOU WALKED *INTO.*

GOT TO *LOVE IT* WHEN THE *NATIVES* GET *RESTLESS.*

HOW LONG IS THIS GOING TO TAKE?

WE'LL HAVE *DISPOSITION* ON THE *SHOOT* TOMORROW, I EXPECT.

IT WAS *RIGHTEOUS,* INSPECTOR.

HOPE- FULLY THAT'S HOW IT'LL CHECK OUT.

IT *WAS* A *CLEAN* SHOOT.

WHAT DO YOU WANT ME TO SAY, DETECTIVE? EVEN *IF* I THINK THAT, I CAN'T SAY IT, NOT YET.

ASK ME AGAIN *TOMORROW.*

ALL RIGHT, SIT HERE AND BE QUIET.

WHERE'M I GONNA GO, FOOL? YOU GOT ME *CUFFED* HERE!

TAKE IT EASY, GARY. WE'LL GET THIS ALL SORTED SOON ENOUGH.

DAMN, I GOT *SHOT*, MAN! I SHOULD BE *HOME* IN *BED.*

INSPECTOR ESPERANZA?

YOUR *SUSPECT* IS HERE.

HE BROUGHT THAT *ATTORNEY*, FINN RICKERT.

JESUS.

FINN RICKERT?

AMBULANCE CHASER.

PUT THEM IN INTERVIEW ONE, PLEASE.

YES, SIR.

YOU ALREADY SIGNED IT.

NO REASON *NOT* TO.

ALL RIGHT.

CAPTAIN SAWYER'S PUT YOU ON ADMIN UNTIL THIS IS *RESOLVED*.

YEAH, SHE TOLD ME.

BETWEEN YOU AND ME, DETECTIVE, YOU'VE GOT NOTHING TO WORRY ABOUT.

JUST PAPERWORK FROM HERE ON OUT.

THAT'S HIM!

THAT'S THE ONE WHO *SHOT* ME, MAN, AND I WAS *HANDCUFFED* AND ALL THAT!

YOU'RE *SURE* ABOUT THAT, GARY?

THE HELL ARE YOU TALKING ABOUT?

I'M TALKING ABOUT *YOU!*

TRYING TO *KILL* A BROTHER WHEN HE'S *HAND-CUFFED!*

THAT'S ENOUGH...

...YOU GOT SOMETHING TO SAY, SAY IT IN THE BOX.

EASY, THERE, INSPECTOR...

...I LIKE TO KEEP MY *LAW-SUITS* AGAINST THE *DEPARTMENT* COMING *ONE* AT A TIME...

...INSTEAD OF ALL AT *ONCE.*

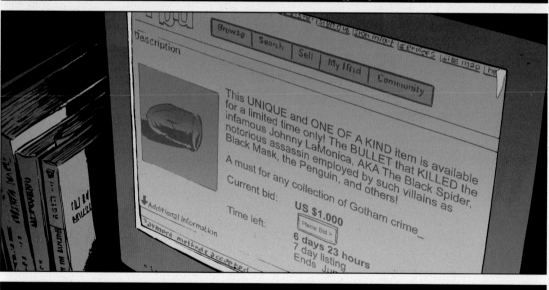

This UNIQUE and ONE OF A KIND item is available for a limited time only! The BULLET that KILLED the infamous Johnny LaMonica, AKA The Black Spider, notorious assassin employed by such villains as Black Mask, the Penguin, and others!

A must for any collection of Gotham crime_

Current bid:

Time left:

US $1.000

6 days 23 hours
7 day listing
Ends Jun

COME TO PAPA.

Police to investigate shooting of handcuffed youth

MCU Detective Allen (left), shown here with partner Detective Renee Montoya

GOTHAM CITY POLICE DEPARTMENT

DATE 6/14/04

WITNESS NAME · LAST, FIRST, M.I.

INITIAL REPORT

RECONSTRUCTION OF OCCURRENCE · SUSPECT NAME/NICKNAME/ALIAS · INCLUDE METHOD OF ENTRY AND ESCAPE · INCLUDE UNIQUE AND UNUSUAL ACTIONS · CLO

DATE/TIME OF OCCUR

Renee Montoya and Crispus Allen are on the Major Crimes Unit's night shift, and Gotham is smack in the middle of a gang war. The two stumble into a firefight between members of the Burnley Town Massive and the infamous assassin, the Black Spider, A.K.A. Johnny LaMonica. Caught in the crossfire, Montoya is hit multiple times by the Black Spider, her bulletproof vest and her partner the only things that spare her life. Allen unloads his weapon into LaMonica, and Gotham is less one costumed freak.

Inspector Manny Esperanza of I.A.D. is brought in to investigate the shooting, and to clear Allen of any wrongdoing. It should be a dunker, but a surviving gang member, Gary Watson, winged in the exchange of fire after he'd been handcuffed, sees a chance to take the City of Gotham for a few million dollars for "pain and suffering." With attorney Finn Rickert's guidance, Watson accuses Allen of the injury.

It shouldn't hold up; it wouldn't hold up, if the evidence were known. But the lead technician who processed the scene is none other than James Corrigan, who has a reputation for making evidence "disappear" normally onto internet auction sites.

The missing bullet, the one that could exonerate Allen, is also the one Corrigan lifted from the scene and put up for sale on iBid. Allen is now on administrative leave until the case is resolved.

For Montoya, who knows she owes her partner her life, there's only one thing for it.

Find the bullet.

POLICE DEPARTMENT OF GOTHAM

Inspector Manuel Esperanza

DOB: 06/09/1959
Eyes: Brown
Rank: Detective
Dept. Internal Affairs

Badge #3585
Height: 6'2"
Weight: 182
Hair Color: Black

JIM CORRIGAN

CORRIGAN PART TWO

HEY, LET ME *HELP.*

UH, *NO,* DORE, YOU JUST *SIT* TIGHT.

WOULDN'T BE MUCH OF AN INVITATION TO *BRUNCH* IF WE LET YOU DO THE *DISHES.*

IT'S THE *DISTRIBUTION* OF *LABOR* AROUND HERE.

YEAH, SHE *COOKS,* I DO THE DISHES.

CRIS, GIVE ME A *HAND?*

WHAT, I DON'T *QUALIFY* AS A *GUEST?*

NO. DEE, YOU SIT, TOO, YOU DID *YOUR* PART.

DON'T CARRY TOO MUCH.

MY *RIBS* ARE *FINE.*

YOUR RIBS ARE *CRACKED,* MY LOVE.

JAKE, MAL, MAKE. YOURSELVES *USEFUL.*

HELP CLEAR THE TABLE.

YOU'VE GOT *GOOD* KIDS.

MOST OF THE TIME.

DO THE *BOYS* KNOW WHAT HAPPENED? ABOUT THE *SHOOTING?*

CRIS AND I TALKED ABOUT IT, DECIDED IT'D BE *BEST* TO TELL THEM.

WITH THE *LAWSUIT* AND *EVERYTHING,* WE DIDN'T WANT THEM TO HEAR ABOUT IT IN THE *NEWS.*

JAKE UNDERSTANDS IT *BETTER,* HE'S ALMOST *SEVENTEEN.* BUT MALCOLM, HE'S FOURTEEN, HE HAD TROUBLE WITH IT.

WE'VE ALWAYS *RAISED* THE BOYS TELLING THEM *VIOLENCE* ISN'T A *SOLUTION.*

CRIS FINALLY TOLD HIM THAT THERE WASN'T *ANY* OTHER *CHOICE.*

HE TOLD HIM THAT LAMONICA WAS ABOUT TO *MURDER* HIS *PARTNER.*

HE WAS TRYING TO *SAVE* RENEE'S *LIFE.*

HE *DID.*

THANKS, GUYS.

THERE'S A *VIDEO GAME* CONSOLE HOOKED UP TO THE TV, IF YOU WANT TO *SAVE* THE *EARTH* FROM AN ALIEN *INVASION* OR SOMETHING.

SICK!

CAN WE, DAD?

YOU MAY.

QUIETLY.

VIDEO GAMES?

THEY'RE DEE'S, I SWEAR.

SURE.

I TALKED TO *ESPERANZA* ON FRIDAY.

HE SAYS FINN RICKERT'S ALL SET TO *DEPOSE* YOU THIS WEEK.

HE SHOULDN'T HAVE TOLD YOU THAT.

IT'S *ALL* BULL$#&*, CRIS. THERE'S NO WAY IN *HELL* YOU COULD HAVE EVEN *HIT* THAT PUNK, WHAT'S HIS NAME?

GARY WATSON.

THE *ANGLE* WAS *TOTALLY* WRONG. IT HAS TO HAVE BEEN ONE OF LAMONICA'S *ROUNDS* THAT *WINGED* HIM.

YEAH.

THAT'S WHAT *I* KEEP SAYING, TOO.

PROBLEM IS, IT'S NOT WHAT EITHER GARY WATSON OR FINN RICKERT IS CLAIMING.

AND THERE'S NO EVIDENCE TO PROVE THEM WRONG AND ME RIGHT.

WHAT, C.S.U. DIDN'T MATCH ALL THE ROUNDS?

C.S.U., RENEE.

THESE GUYS LIFT A CLEAN PRINT, WE'RE LUCKY. YOU HONESTLY SURPRISED THAT THEY MISSED A COUPLE OF BULLETS?

HERE, USE THIS.

THANKS.

WHO WAS THE LEAD TECH?

CORRIGAN.

JESUS.

THERE'S YOUR PROBLEM.

TELL ME ABOUT IT.

BUT WHILE YOU AND ME AND MAYBE HALF THE M.C.U. KNOW HE'S ROTTEN...

...AIN'T NOBODY GOT PROOF THAT IT'S SO.

HEY, JO, GOT A MINUTE?

YOU GOTTA MAKE IT FAST, RENEE, MARCUS AND I HAVE TO *SERVE* A *WARRANT* ON THE RIDDLER THING.

YOU MAKING AN *ARREST?*

NAH, JUST A *SEARCH.* WHAT'S UP?

YOU KNOW CORRIGAN IN C.S.U., RIGHT?

JIMMY? *I KNOW* HIM, YEAH.

IT'S NOT LIKE WE'RE BUNKIES OR ANYTHING.

OKAY.

BECAUSE I HEARD YOU WERE *BANGING* THE *GUY.*

WHO THE *HELL* TOLD YOU *THAT?* DID MARCUS TELL YOU THAT?

NO, IT WASN'T DRIVER.

THEN *WHERE* THE *HELL* DO YOU GET OFF ASKING ME A QUESTION LIKE THAT?

IT'S JUST SOMETHING I HEARD, THAT'S ALL.

SO IT'S *CURIOSITY?* THAT'S IT?

SORRY TO *DISAPPOINT* YOU RENEE, BUT I *DON'T* PLAY FOR *YOUR* TEAM.

SOMEHOW I *MANAGE* TO SLEEP THROUGH THE NIGHT *ANYWAY.*

WHY'RE YOU ASKING ABOUT *CORRIGAN?*

BECAUSE I THINK THE *ROTTEN* SON OF A BITCH IS RESPONSIBLE FOR DROPPING MY *PARTNER* IN THE *JACKPOT.*

AND IF YOU *WERE* SLEEPING WITH HIM, MAYBE YOU'D *KNOW* SOMETHING ABOUT THAT.

&#$* YOU.

YOU WANT TO *ACCUSE* ME OF SOMETHING, MONTOYA, YA DO IT IN THE *BOX.*

OTHERWISE, KEEP THE *HELL* OUT OF MY *FACE.*

DETECTIVE MONTOYA.

SOMEONE PISSED IN DETECTIVE MACDONALD'S CORNFLAKES, IT SEEMS.

WHAT DO YOU *WANT*, ESPERANZA?

JUST SAYING HELLO.

WELL, *THAT* AND WONDERING IF IT WAS *YOU* WHO SET OFF MAC.

SHE TOOK *UMBRAGE* AT AN *INQUIRY* I MADE.

UMBRAGE. THAT'S A *GREAT* WORD, *UMBRAGE*.

AND WHAT CAUSED HER TO... *UMBER*?

I'D HEARD SHE AND CORRIGAN HAD A *THING*. WANTED TO SEE IF IT WAS *TRUE*.

IT *ISN'T*.

HELL, *I* COULD HAVE TOLD YOU *THAT*, MONTOYA. HE'S GOT A PIECE OVER AT *FINNIGAN'S*. YOU KNOW FINNIGAN'S, RIGHT, DETECTIVE?

OVER BY THE WESTERN. IT'S A *COP* BAR, IF WE *DEFINE* "COP" TO MEAN THAT *MAJORITY* OF THE G.C.P.D. ...

...WHO THINK CARRYING A *BADGE* IS AN *EXCUSE* TO LINE THEIR OWN *POCKETS*...

...SERIOUSLY CHERRY, YOU HAVE TO SEE THIS BABY, MADE TO PURR...

HEY, GINA! TWO MORE PITCHERS AND SOME PRETZELS!

...MAKING TIME-AND-A-*HALF* ON THIS IS A *GOLD MINE*...

...TAKE A LOOK AT THAT...

...SO *THAT* WAS ON TUESDAY, RIGHT? THEN ON WEDNESDAY, WE GET THE SAME CALL *AGAIN*...

--DAMN *DOMESTIC*, SO I STARTED USING MY *STICK* ON THEM *BOTH*...

SURE, I'M *ON DUTY*, BUT MY *SERGEANT* KNOWS I'M HERE.

--ABOUT HOW I'M NEVER HOME, SO I SHOW HER THE *BACK* OF MY *HAND*--

...NAH, NOT ANYMORE, BUT I'VE GOT A LITTLE S&W THAT I CARRY NOW AS A BACK-UP...

...NO, THE *OTHER* ONE, THE ONE IN *TRI-CORNER*, WITH THE *ORIENTAL* CHICKS...

--I.A.D. *BASTARD*, TOLD HIM HE WANTED TO HEAR MORE, TO CALL MY *UNION* REP!

...*HOT* LITTLE NUMBER, SO I TELL HER I *COULD* RIP THE *TICKET* BUT...

--HASN'T *PAID* UP YET, THINKING A *VISIT* MIGHT BE IN *ORDER*...

LOOKS LIKE SOME-BODY GOT LOST.

M.C.U. DYKE.

CORRIGAN.

DETECTIVE MONTOYA.

YOU GET *LOST* OR SOMETHING?

I THOUGHT YOU M.C.U. TYPES WERE TOO *GOOD* TO DRINK WITH THE *WORKING CLASS.*

I'VE GOT SOME *QUESTIONS* FOR YOU ABOUT THE LAMONICA CRIME SCENE.

YOU CAN *READ* MY *REPORT.*

YOUR REPORT HAS SOME *HOLES* IN IT.

BULLET- SIZED ONES.

OH, WOW, THAT'S *CLEVER.*

*BULLET-*SIZED ONES.

THERE ARE *ROUNDS* UNACCOUNTED FOR.

YOUR *REPORT* SAYS YOU RECOVERED *THIRTY-THREE* FROM THE SCENE.

BUT *BALLISTICS* ONLY HAS *THIRTY-TWO* OF THEM.

I *MISCOUNTED.*

RIGHT.

SO I GUESS *THAT* MEANS YOU'RE NOT ONLY *CROOKED,* YOU'RE *STUPID,* AS WELL.

I'D *BE* CAREFUL WHAT YOU'RE *SAYING,* DETECTIVE.

WHAT WITH YOU HAVING *CRACKED* RIBS AND *NO* BACKUP.

YOU WANT TO TAKE THIS *OUTSIDE,* JIMMY?

I'D BE *GLAD* TO TAKE THIS *OUTSIDE.*

YOU'RE *WEARING* YOUR PIECE, YOU NEED TO DITCH IT, DYKE.

I DON'T WANT YOU *SHOOTING* ME WHEN YOU *LOSE.*

CAN I SHOOT YOU WHEN I *WIN?*

HOLD THESE.

SEE HOW *ARROGANT* YOU ARE WITH *BROKEN* TEETH!

HNNFFF.

NGH.

AAAAHHHH!

UNNHHH

HOW'RE THOSE RIBS--

--YOU STUCK UP--

--SELF-RIGHTEOUS--

45

...JUST SAW *ME* HAND YOU YOUR *ASS.*

NOW, YOU GONNA COME *CLEAN,* OR AM I GONNA *BEAT* YOU SOME *MORE?*

GIVE IT SOME *THOUGHT,* JIMMY...

...BECAUSE I CAN DO THIS *ALL NIGHT...*

HE GIVE IT UP?

YOU FOLLOW ME?

DID HE GIVE IT UP, DETECTIVE?

HOW MUCH DID YOU SEE?

ENOUGH.

HE SOLD IT TO SOME COLLECTOR OUT IN THE 'BURBS FOR ALMOST TEN GRAND.

NAME OF JENNIFER GORDON-HEWITT.

THEN I'LL VISIT MS. HEWITT IN THE MORNING.

LIKE HELL.

YOU USE ME TO BREAK DOWN CORRIGAN, YOU DON'T GET TO CUT ME OUT AT THE END, INSPECTOR.

I'LL MEET YOU AT CENTRAL IN THE MORNING...

...WE CAN TALK TO MS. HEWITT TOGETHER.

OH, RENEE... YOU SHOULD SEE THE *OTHER* GUY.

IT'S *NOT* FUNNY!

I KNOW.

I DON'T *LIKE* THIS, I DON'T LIKE *YOU* LIKE THIS!

WOULD YOU *RATHER* I LIED?

NO, OF COURSE *NOT!*

I *KNOW* IT'S... IT'S A *VIOLENT* CITY...

...IT'S A VIOLENT *JOB*, EVEN...

...IT'S JUST...SOME-TIMES...

...SOMETIMES I THINK YOU *LIKE* THAT IT'S *VIOLENT*...

I DID WHAT I HAD TO *DO*.

I *GOT* WHAT I WAS AFTER.

EACH TO THEIR **ABILITES.**

LET ME DO THE TALKING.

YOU TRUST ME TO **BEAT** CORRIGAN, BUT NOT TO OPEN MY **MOUTH?**

WHAT'S **THAT** SUPPOSED TO MEAN?

YOU'RE A **DETECTIVE,** YOU FIGURE IT OUT.

I DON'T LIKE BEING **USED.**

I DIDN'T **MAKE** YOU DO **ANYTHING** YOU DIDN'T **WANT** TO, RENEE.

DONG DONG DONG

INSPECTOR MANUEL ESPERANZA, G.C.P.D., THIS IS DETECTIVE MONTOYA.

WERE LOOKING FOR JENNIFER GORDON-HEWITT.

OH, DEAR...

...THIS IS ABOUT THE **SCALPELS**, ISN'T IT?

I BOUGHT THEM IN **GOOD FAITH**, I WAS **ASSURED** THAT HE'D **NEVER** ACTUALLY GOTTEN AROUND TO **USING** THEM.

IMAGINE MY **SURPRISE** WHEN I **REALIZED** THERE WAS **DRIED BLOOD** ON THE **HANDLES**, I MEAN, I NEVER !

OH, DEAR.

OH, DEAR OH, DEAR OH, DEAR ME.

SCALPELS?

PERHAPS YOU'D BETTER COME IN.

PERHAPS WE'D **BETTER.**

SCALPELS?

FOR MY ZSASZ SECTION, YES. I'VE **SEVERAL** PIECES DETAILING HIS **CAREER** IN MY **COLLECTION,** ACTUALLY.

YOUR **COLLECTION** OF...?

CRIME MEMORABILIA. IT'S MY **PASSION,** ESPECIALLY THE ITEMS AND OBJECTS OF GOTHAM'S MORE **NEFARIOUS** CRIMINALS.

THAT'S WHY YOU'RE **HERE,** I'M SURE. TO **VIEW** MY **COLLECTION.**

OF COURSE.

THOUGHT SO.

I KEEP THE **MAJORITY** IN HERE...

...BUT THERE'S *MUCH* MORE IN *STORAGE,* TOO.

IT WAS MY *LATE* HUSBAND WHO *STARTED* THE COLLECTION, OF COURSE. HE SAW THE BATMAN ONCE, FIGHTING THAT *CROCODILE* FELLOW.

AS *HE* TOLD IT--GOD REST HIS SOUL-- BATMAN GAVE THAT PERPETRATOR A *MIGHTY* WALLOP, AND JUST LIKE *THAT,* ONE OF THOSE CROCODILE *TEETH* FLEW OUT OF HIS MOUTH.

LANDED RIGHT IN BARTHOLOMEW'S *LAP,* IT DID...

...THAT'S WHAT *STARTED* IT, OF COURSE. HE BROUGHT IT *HOME* AND *CLEANED* IT UP.

IT'S STILL *AROUND* HERE, SOMEWHERE, I THINK I COULD *DIG* IT OUT FOR YOU, IF YOU--

ACTUALLY, WE'RE LOOKING FOR A *BULLET* YOU PURCHASED *RECENTLY.*

WELL, DEAR... I'VE PURCHASED A *LOT* OF BULLETS, RECENTLY.

THIS *GANG WAR'S* BEEN A *BONANZA,* I'VE HAD TO SELL SOME *STOCK* JUST TO--

THIS IS FROM THE BLACK SPIDER KILLING.

SPENT A *PRETTY* PENNY ON *THAT*.

WELL, WE'LL BE *TAKING* IT WITH US.

NO, NO, DEAR, I *DON'T* THINK YOU *WILL*, NOT WITHOUT A *WARRANT* OF SOME SORT.

IT'S *MINE* FROM A *LEGAL* AND *LEGITIMATE* TRANSACTION.

IT'S *EVIDENCE* OF A *CRIME*--

OF COURSE IT IS, THAT'S WHY I BOUGHT IT.

--BUT *NOT* THE CRIME YOU *THINK*.

THE *BULLET* YOU BOUGHT *DIDN'T* KILL LAMONICA, MRS. HEWITT.

THE *SELLER* CLAIMED--

YEAH, HE *LIED*.

TELL YOU WHAT, WE'LL *TRADE* YOU FOR IT.

TRADE?

SURE. YOU WANTED A PIECE OF BLACK SPIDER MEMORABILIA, WELL, I'VE *GOT* ONE, AND IT'S *UNIQUE*...

...TAKEN RIGHT FROM MY VEST...

...THE *LAST* BULLET JOHNNY LAMONICA EVER *FIRED*...

YOU'LL RUN THE **SLUG** DOWN TO THE **LAB** WHEN WE GET BACK.

YEAH, IF IT'S FROM ALLEN'S **GUN** LIKE WE FIGURE, THAT'LL BE THAT.

JUST KEEP IT AWAY FROM **CORRIGAN**, THAT'S ALL I **ASK**.

I SUSPECT CORRIGAN'S GONNA BE ON HIS **BEST** BEHAVIOR, EVEN **IF** THAT BOY'S ROTTEN TO THE **CORE**.

HE'S GONNA BE **UNTOUCHABLE**, NOW, YOU KNOW THAT.

ANYTHING YOU GET ON HIM, IT'S ALL FRUIT FROM THE **POISON** TREE.

I KNOW.

THEN **WHY'D** YOU TURN ME LOOSE ON HIM, INSPECTOR?

YOUR **PARTNER** WAS IN THE **JACKPOT**, MONTOYA. I COULDN'T LET THAT **SIT**.

SO YOU LET ME **KILL** YOUR **CASE** AGAINST CORRIGAN TO GET HIM OUT?

I DON'T **BELIEVE** YOU.

WHY'D YOU **DO** IT?

BECAUSE I **OWED** YOU ONE.

LET'S GIVE YOUR PARTNER THE **GOOD** NEWS.

THE END

LIGHTS OUT

Written by
GREG RUCKA

Art by
MICHAEL LARK & STEFANO GAUDIANO

Colors by
LEE LOUGHRIDGE

Letters by
CLEM ROBINS

The apparent assassination of Gotham's top gang leaders led to all out war between the criminal factions of the city. As bodies began to drop faster and faster, the G.C.P.D. found itself stretched to its limits, its officers caught in the crossfire between the criminals and the Batman, who—to the eyes of the G.C.P.D. and Police Commissioner Michael Akins—seemed to view the police as his own private army.

This view was reinforced when Batman ignored police control of a hostage situation at the Louis H. Grieve Memorial High School, leading to the death of one student, and, later, commandeering control of the police band, in an attempt to issue direct orders to the G.C.P.D. The result was a disaster that left numerous officers wounded, and over two-dozen killed at the hands of Gotham's criminal element....

JUST *THREE* OF YOU?

THE *WORK* ORDER SAID IT WAS *ROUTINE* MAINTENANCE, COMMISSIONER.

YOU *WANT*, I CAN GO BACK OVER TO CITY HALL AND MAKE A *REQUEST* FOR MORE.

AND HOW *LONG* WILL *THAT* TAKE?

WELL, YOU'D HAVE TO FILL OUT THE E-SEVENTY-TWO *AGAIN*, AND THEN A *SUPPLEMENTAL* FORM, Y'KNOW, *EXPLAINING* THE *CHANGE*...

FIGURE, MAYBE TWO, THREE WEEKS?

NO, I'M NOT *WAITING* ANY LONGER.

I WANT THIS *DONE* BY TONIGHT.

THEN ALL YOU GOT TO DO IS *TELL* US WHAT THE *JOB* IS.

THAT.

TAKE IT DOWN.

I WANT IT *GONE* BY *NIGHTFALL.*

HEY, WAIT A *SECOND!*

WHAT?

WHAT DO WE DO WITH IT WHEN WE'RE *DONE?*

I DON'T GIVE A DAMN.

I THINK *AKINS* IS OFF HIS *NUT.*

WELL, HE HASN'T *FIRED* YOU YET, SO THERE'S *EVIDENCE* TO *SUPPORT* THAT THEORY, TOMMY.

THANKS, DAG. THAT'S THE KIND OF *BACKUP* I WAS HOPING FOR FROM MY *PARTNER.*

SERIOUSLY, MAN, WHAT'S HE *THINKING,* TAKING THE *SIGNAL* DOWN AND ALL?

LIKE IT'S GONNA STOP THAT *LUNATIC* FROM *MESSING* IN OUR *BUSINESS* ANYWAY.

THE COMMISSIONER IS MAKING A *STATEMENT,* DETECTIVE BURKE...

...*ANNOUNCING* IN NO UNCERTAIN TERMS THAT THE *G.C.P.D.* AND THE *BATMAN* ARE NO LONGER ON SPEAKING TERMS.

MAYBE.

OR MAYBE HE'S JUST *ANNOUNCED* TO EVERY *INMATE* AT ARKHAM THAT GOTHAM IS NOW *EASY PICKINGS.*

WHICH CAME *FIRST?*

THE *BATMAN* OR THE *FREAKS?*

THE BATMAN **IS** ONE OF THE **FREAKS.**

SOMETHING THAT YOU **NATIVE** GOTHAMITES SEEM TO **FORGET.**

NO, HE'S **NOT.**

NO?

NO.

HE **SAVES** LIVES. HE **PROTECTS** THE PEOPLE WE **CAN'T.**

YEAH, HE **SAVED** LOTS OF **LIVES** WHEN HE TOOK OVER THE **POLICE BAND.**

HE DID A BANG-UP JOB WHEN WE HAD BLACK MASK **SURROUNDED.**

HOW **MANY** COPS DIED IN THIS **GANG WAR?** TWENTY-SIX? TWENTY-SEVEN?

MORE THAN **THAT.**

OFFICER ACEDILLO **DIED** LAST NIGHT FROM THE **INJURIES** HE GOT IN ROBINSON PARK.

THAT SOUND LIKE A **HERO** TO YOU, RENEE?

BECAUSE I'M **PRETTY** SURE ROMY WOULD **DISAGREE.**

NICE **SHOT,** THERE, CRIS.

SHOVE IT, BURKE.

CAPTAIN SAWYER! MAGGIE! MAGS!

MAGS?

DIDN'T *LIKE* THAT ONE, HUH?

WHAT CAN I DO FOR YOU, SIMON?

YOU CAN *SLOW* DOWN FOR A START.

MAKE IT *FAST*, I'VE GOT SOMEWHERE TO BE.

EARLY *LUNCH?*

DOCTOR'S APPOINTMENT.

WHAT DO YOU *NEED?*

YOU GOT A *COMMENT* ABOUT WHAT'S GOING ON UP ON THE *ROOF?*

STACY *ALWAYS* HAS LUNCH UP THERE, SIMON. UNLESS THE *WEATHER'S* BAD.

SERIOUSLY.

THE *DEPARTMENT* HAS NO *OFFICIAL* COMMENT OR *POSITION* ON BATMAN, AND THAT *INCLUDES* THE *SIGNAL*, YOU KNOW THAT.

YEAH, I *KNOW* THE *POLICY.*

I'M ASKING FOR A *COMMENT* OFF THE *RECORD.*

IT'D HAVE TO BE *WAY* OFF THE RECORD.

HAVE I *EVER* TREATED YOU OR YOUR PEOPLE *WRONG*, CAPTAIN?

YOU *KNOW* I DON'T GIVE UP MY *SOURCES.*

YOU *KNOW* WHAT HAPPENED, SIMON.

HE *SCREWED* US.

WHAT *ELSE* IS AKINS SUPPOSED TO *DO?*

DUDE, CHECK *HER* OUT...

...WOULDN'T *MIND* GETTING SOME OF *THAT.*

HEY, SUGARLEGS!

HOPE YOU BROUGHT *ENOUGH* TO *SHARE,* SEXY!

C'MERE, I'LL *SHOW* YOU WHAT I *GOT* IN *MY* LUNCHBOX!

NAH, *DON'T* GO!

OW!

¢#$%HOLE.

ROOF ACCESS
AUTHORIZED PERSONNEL ONLY

...THEN JUST CUT OUT THE DAMN *MIDDLEMAN* AND START HANDING OUT *BADGES* TO THE GENERAL *POPULACE!*

WHAT YOU SEEM TO FORGET IS THAT THIS GUY IS A *VIGILANTE!*

AND THE DEPARTMENT'S *ENTIRE* RELATIONSHIP WITH THIS GUY WAS BUILT ON *ONE* SIMPLE *TRUST--*

AND HE *BROKE* IT!

YOU CAN'T *BLAME* HIM FOR *EVERY* LIFE THAT WAS *LOST,* CRIS!

I DON'T *HAVE* TO! ALL I HAVE TO DO IS BLAME HIM FOR *ONE!*

AND YOU'LL *FORGIVE* ME FOR SAYING THIS, *PARTNER,* BUT YOU'RE ABOUT AS OBJECTIVE ON THIS AS THE *POPE* IS ON THE SUBJECT OF *ABORTION.*

BITE ME, CRIS.

WHEN THE *POLICE* WORK WITH A *LAWBREAKER,* THE POLICE *LOSE* THE FAITH OF THE PUBLIC!

MAYBE YOU HAVEN'T NOTICED, BUT WE'VE NEVER *HAD* THE FAITH OF THE PUBLIC!

HE'S *NOT* A COP, HE'S *NEVER* BEEN A *COP--*

AND *THINKING* HE WAS ON OUR *SIDE* GOT PEOPLE *KILLED!*

JUST WHAT THE *HELL* ARE YOU *DOING?*

I BEG YOUR *PARDON*, MISTER *MAYOR?*

I ASKED WHAT THE *HELL* YOU'RE *DOING*, MIKE!

YOU DON'T MAKE A *DECISION* LIKE THIS WITHOUT *CONSULTING* WITH ME *FIRST!*

ASIDE FROM THE *FACT* THAT I LOOKED LIKE AN *ASS* AT THE *PRESS CONFERENCE* THIS MORNING, YOU DON'T HAVE THE *AUTHORITY* TO MAKE THIS KIND OF DECISION!

GCPD to Bat: Go to Hell!

Mayor Hull: "No Comment!"

YOU HAVE *ANY* IDEA HOW THIS MAKES ME *LOOK?*

NOT TO *MENTION* WHAT IT'S GOING TO DO TO THE *TOURISM* INDUSTRY IN THIS CITY?

I COULD CARE *LESS* ABOUT WHAT IT DOES TO *TOURISM.*

THIS IS ABOUT PROTECTING MY PEOPLE, AND BATMAN IS A *MENACE.*

YOU'RE THE COMMISSIONER OF POLICE, YOU HAD *DAMN* WELL BETTER CARE ABOUT *TOURISM!*

THE *HEALTH* AND *WELFARE* OF GOTHAM CITY IS YOUR *CONCERN*, COMMISSIONER.

PUT IT *BACK.*

NO.

YOU WANT ME TO *FIRE* YOU, MIKE? IS THAT WHAT YOU *WANT*?

BECAUSE I'LL BE *GLAD* TO *DO* IT.

I'VE GOT NO PROBLEM SENDING YOU *PACKING* AND FINDING ANOTHER *COP* WHO'LL ACTUALLY *LISTEN* TO ME.

THAT'S YOUR *CHOICE.*

BUT I'D THINK *TWICE* ABOUT MAKING A *MOVE* LIKE THAT, MISTER MAYOR...

...ESPECIALLY WHEN *MY* DEPARTMENT IS INVESTIGATING *YOUR* OFFICE FOR *CORRUPTION.*

WHAT?

SINCE *WHEN?*

SINCE YOU TOOK THAT *LEXCORP-* SPONSORED *TRIP* TO THE *CAYMANS* AND LEFT *MRS. HULL* HERE AT *HOME.*

YOU WANT TO *CALL MY BLUFF?*

NO.

DIDN'T *THINK* SO.

NOW, YOU'LL *EXCUSE* ME...

...I'VE GOT AN *OFFICER'S* FUNERAL TO *ATTEND.*

...EASY...

...DAMMIT, I SAID EASY!

SORRY!

JUST WATCH THE SLACK, WILL YOU?

WE'RE GONNA SET IT OVER THERE, ALL RIGHT?

GOT IT.

JUST A LITTLE FURTHER...

AH, DAMMIT!

I WAS TRYING TO DO **HOMEWORK,** BUT I COULDN'T **CONCENTRATE.**

THERE'D BEEN THIS **STORY** IN THE **NEWS,** HOW THE **WATER SUPPLY** HAD BEEN **POISONED.**

EVERYONE IN THE **CITY** WAS **SCARED.**

I LOOKED OUT MY **WINDOW.**

DETECTIVE **ALLEN?**

YOUR **TURN** ON THE **STAND.**

RIGHT.

THANKS.

STACY?

CAPTAIN! I WASN'T--I MEAN, I DIDN'T...

IT'S **ALL** RIGHT.

BUT YOU **CAN'T** BE UP HERE.

NOT ANY-MORE.

I KNOW.

HE'S **NOT** A BAD GUY, CAPTAIN.

WE **KNOW** WHO THE **BAD** GUYS ARE, HE'S **NOT** ONE OF **THEM.**

I KNOW.

'NIGHT, COMMISSIONER.

GOOD NIGHT.

TURN *AROUND.*

WONDERED WHEN YOU'D COME TO *BUST* MY CHOPS.

YOU'RE MAKING A *MISTAKE.*

FROM WHERE I'M *STANDING,* I'M *CORRECTING* ONE.

TAKING DOWN THE *SIGNAL* DOESN'T *CHANGE* ANYTHING.

I'LL *STILL* DO WHAT I NEED TO *DO.*

YOU MAY BE *RIGHT.*

BUT THIS WAY, AT LEAST, THERE WON'T BE ANY MORE CONFUSION.

THIS WAY, AT LEAST, MY PEOPLE WON'T MAKE THE MISTAKE OF THINKING THAT YOU'RE ON THEIR SIDE.

WE'RE ON THE SAME SIDE, COMMISSIONER.

NO, WE'RE NOT.

WE BOTH WANT TO PROTECT GOTHAM.

WE BOTH WANT TO KEEP ITS PEOPLE SAFE.

THAT'S WHAT I WANT.

BUT I DON'T THINK THAT'S WHAT YOU WANT.

WHAT ELSE COULD THERE BE?

I DON'T KNOW.

I DON'T KNOW WHY YOU DO WHAT YOU DO. IF IT'S ABOUT POWER OR EGO OR REVENGE...

...MAYBE JUST FOR KICKS...

FRANKLY, I DON'T CARE ANYMORE.

THE SIGNAL WAS THERE BECAUSE ONCE UPON A TIME THE G.C.P.D. TRUSTED YOU. WELL...

...THAT TIME HAS PASSED.

THE END

ON THE FREAK BEAT

Written by
ED BRUBAKER

Art by
JASON ALEXANDER

Colors by
LEE LOUGHRIDGE

Letters by
CLEM ROBINS

GOTHAM CITY, DECEMBER 10TH.

--HOW MANY TIMES I'VE HAD TO TELL THIS MORON THAT HOMICIDE INVESTIGATIONS ARE **NOT** LIKE NARCO BUSTS.

ALWAYS REACHING FOR HIS PIECE LIKE WE'RE ABOUT TO BLOW THE DOOR OFF SOME CRACK HOUSE OR METH LAB.

IT WAS FUNNY AT FIRST, BUT **NOW** IT'S JUST ANNOYING.

I MEAN, YOU WALK INTO THE GOTHAM GENTLEMAN'S CLUB TO INTERVIEW J. WUTHERINGTON THE FOURTH, AND YOUR PARTNER'S WAVING A GUN AROUND LIKE IT'S THE WILD FRIGGIN' WEST.

DOES **NOT** GO OVER TOO WELL, LET ME TELL YOU.

I CAN **IMAGINE**, ROMY...

...THAT WAS ONE THING ABOUT CHARLIE THAT **ALWAYS** REASSURED ME. UNTIL THE DAY HE DIED, I THINK HE ONLY FIRED HIS GUN **ONCE** IN THE LINE OF DUTY.

HE WAS ALWAYS SAYING, "DON'T WORRY, I SHOW UP AFTER ALL THE SHOOTING'S DONE."

YOU'RE DONE WITH THIS?

LET ME GET THESE, NORA, YOU **COOKED**...

DON'T BE RIDICULOUS, DEAR. THIS IS **MY** HOME, I CAN TAKE CARE OF MY GUESTS.

MARCUS, I CAN TAKE *YOUR* PLATE, OR ARE YOU GOING TO TRY TO DO ALL THE HEAVY LIFTING FOR THE *CRIPPLE,* TOO?

HEH, *NO...* I FELL FOR THAT NONSENSE AT THANKSGIVING AND WOUND UP IN THERE FOR TWO HOURS WHILE *YOU TWO* WATCHED THE GAME.

GAME?

YEAH, WE WATCHED THE *TWILIGHT ZONE* MARATHON. #€%$ THE *GAME.*

HEY, NOW I'M *REALLY* BURNED.

SO, NORA, I'VE REALLY BEEN MEANING TO ASK...SINCE YOU'RE ONLY CUTTING UP *DEAD PEOPLE,* CAN YOU STILL *WORK* WITH THE PROSTHETIC?

Y'KNOW, I NEVER THOUGHT TO TRY. I JUST TOOK THE PROMOTION TO SUPERVISOR AND FELT A WAVE OF RELIEF.

TEN YEARS IS ENOUGH TIME IN A MORGUE, DON'T YOU THINK?

BLEEDEL-DEET

OH, WHAT THE HELL? I'M ON IN AN HOUR ALREADY...

DRIVER HERE.

UH HUNH... YEAH...

DAMN IT, JOSIE...WHAT'VE I TOLD YOU ABOUT SHOWING UP FOR SHIFT EARLY?

PAPERWORK, RIGHT...BLAH BLAH BLAH...

YOU'RE SITTING AT A DESK, YOU'RE GONNA PICK UP A CASE.

WHAT IS IT?

BODY IN A PENTHOUSE, *UPTOWN*...

NO, NO... IT'S OKAY, JOSIE. I'LL MEET YOU THERE.

GET ROMY TO DROP ME.

SORRY TO CUT OUT ON YOU LIKE THIS, NORA.

I KNOW THE ROUTINE, DETECTIVE DRIVER, I *DON'T* NEED AN APOLOGY.

SURE, AND BESIDES, YOU'VE GOT ALL THESE *DISHES* TO KEEP YOU BUSY.

AND DON'T FORGET MY *STORIES* ARE ALL ON THE TIVO.

BYE, NORA, SEE YOU NEXT WEEK.

OF COURSE, DEAR. TAKE CARE OF HIM.

I ALWAYS DO.

WHAT?

NOTHING. SHE'S JUST AMAZING.

YEAH, CHARLIE HAD GREAT TASTE.

SO, YOU GOT AN *ADDRESS* ON THIS BODY?

83

On The **Freak Beat**

HEY JOSIE, WHAT'S WITH ALL THE TV PEOPLE SWARMING AROUND HERE?

AH, THE DOORMAN OR SOMEONE LEAKED THE NAME A WHILE BACK AND IT'S BEEN A MADHOUSE EVER SINCE.

COMMISSIONER AKINS IS ON HIS WAY DOWN, GONNA MAKE SOME KIND OF STATEMENT.

WHO WAS OUR VIC? ANYBODY I KNOW?

YOU A BORN-AGAIN CHRISTIAN?

IS THAT **RELEVANT**?

WOULD'VE BEEN TO HIM...

...MEET THE **LATE** REVEREND BUFORD PRESSMAN.

WAIT, THE **TELEVANGELIST** GUY?

GOT IT IN ONE.

I **HATE** THAT GUY.

COOL, GOT MY FIRST SUSPECT ALREADY.

WE GOT A *TIME OF DEATH* YET?

MIKE?

WELL...DON'T *QUOTE* ME ON IT YET, BUT WE'RE LOOKING AT SOMEWHERE BETWEEN ONE AND THREE A.M. LAST NIGHT.

CAUSE?

GUNSHOT WOUND TO THE CHEST. SINGLE SHOT.

DID A QUICK WALK-THROUGH BEFORE YOU GOT HERE, SO TELL ME WHAT THIS LOOKS LIKE TO *YOU*, DRIVER.

WE GOT THE OPEN WALL-SAFE IN THE DEN THERE...

...THREE BULLET HOLES IN THE WALL AND DOORFRAME HERE...

...SIGN OF A STRUGGLE, AND THE REV ON THE FLOOR IN THE ADJOINING ROOM.

A .38 LYING TEN OR SO FEET FROM THE BODY.

SIMPLE. INTERRUPTS A BURGLARY, GRABS HIS GUN AND GETS OFF A FEW SHOTS, BUT THE PERP GETS THE GUN AWAY AND SENDS OUR VIC TO THE HOLY GHOST AHEAD OF SCHEDULE.

BASICALLY.

UNFORTUNATELY, IT'S NOT QUITE *THAT* SIMPLE.

WHAT AM I MISSING?

TWO THINGS. CHECK OUT THE REV'S *FACE*.

SCRATCHES... BUT NOT *TORN* LIKE NAILS. MORE LIKE LITTLE *BLADES*.

RIGHT, AND THEN WE'VE GOT THE SECURITY SYSTEM THAT WAS SHUT DOWN FROM *OUTSIDE* SOMEHOW...

...AND A *POINT OF ENTRY* THAT'S FORTY-FIVE STORIES ABOVE GROUND WITH *NO LEDGE*.

AH, HELL. YOU GOTTA BE *KIDDING* ME.

CATWOMAN?

LOOK AT THIS.

THOSE *EMERALDS*?

I'M NOT AN EXPERT, BUT THAT'S WHAT *I'D* SAY, YEAH.

SO, SHE GETS *INTERRUPTED*, GETS IN A SCUFFLE, SHOOTS THE GUY AND ENDS UP LEAVING SOME JEWELS ON THE CARPET.

PROBABLY *DROPPED* THEM WHEN HE OPENED FIRE.

SHE'S GONNA LEAVE WITHOUT EVERYTHING SHE *CAME FOR*? THE REVEREND'S ALREADY DEAD, AND IF SHE CHECKED OUT THIS PLACE, SHE KNOWS IT'S SOUND-PROOF.

HELL, NO ONE EVEN FOUND THE *BODY* UNTIL TWO HOURS AGO, WHEN HIS SECRETARY CAME LOOKING FOR HIM.

CATWOMAN'S A PRO. I DON'T SEE HER LEAVING GEMS ON THE FLOOR AND RUNNING OFF SCATTER-BRAINED.

TALKING YOURSELF OUT OF YOUR *OWN* THEORY?

JUST A LITTLE. YOU'RE *RIGHT*, THOUGH, SHE NEVER *HAS* KILLED ANYONE, FAR AS I KNOW.

SO, MAYBE SHE FREAKED OUT AND RAN OFF, BUT STILL...

WHAT'S WRONG *NOW*?

I DON'T THINK THAT JEWELRY WAS ACTUALLY *IN* THAT SAFE. I THINK IT WAS *PLANTED*.

WHAT'S THIS, ANOTHER ONE OF YOUR *FEELINGS*? OR WOULD THERE BE SOME *EVIDENCE* INVOLVED THIS TIME?

WHAT'S *THAT* SUPPOSED TO MEAN?

YOU *DON'T* KNOW?

LOOK, ALL I'M SAYING IS...IT'S JUST A LITTLE, UH, *CONVENIENT.* CAN'T I GO WITH MY GUT, OR IS THAT JUST RESERVED FOR THE *OLD SCHOOL* COPS?

NO, YOU *CAN,* I JUST THINK IT'S ODD THAT YOU'D LOOK AT EVIDENCE AND--

TELL ME SOMETHING *GOOD,* DETECTIVES, PLEASE.

COMMISSIONER AKINS. I DON'T, UH, WELL... THERE REALLY ISN'T MUCH GOOD *TO* TELL, HONESTLY.

IT'S LOOKING LIKE *CATWOMAN* RIGHT NOW, SIR, BUT WE'RE NOT A HUNDRED PERCENT ON THAT.

OH, LORD... THAT'S *JUST* WHAT WE NEED, ISN'T IT?

ESPECIALLY *THESE* DAYS.

IT *IS* POSSIBLE THE BAT WILL BRING HER IN WITHOUT BEING *ASKED,* IF SHE'S GUILTY.

IF THAT'S A JOKE, DETECTIVE, IT *ISN'T* FUNNY.

EITHER OF YOU EVER *WATCH* THIS MAN ON TV?

NOT IF I CAN HELP IT.

I GET MY CHURCH IN CHURCH, SIR.

ARE THERE ANY *OTHER* POSSIBLES *BESIDES* CATWOMAN?

WE'RE BRINGING THE WIFE AND A FEW OF HIS ASSOCIATES DOWN TO CENTRAL TO HEAR WHAT THEY'VE GOT TO *SAY*, BUT AT THIS POINT IT'S WHAT YOU *SEE*, COMMISSIONER.

LET'S JUST KEEP A *LID* ON THIS WHOLE CATWOMAN ANGLE FOR THE *TIME BEING*, THEN.

AN IMPORTANT *COMMUNITY LEADER* GETS KILLED, LAST THING WE NEED IS TO SEE THE *FREAK ANGLE* PLAY OUT IN THE NEWS.

NOW I'VE GOT TO GO GIVE THESE VULTURES SOMETHING TO CHEW ON FOR THEIR NEXT NEWS-CYCLE. KEEP ME UPDATED ON YOUR PROGRESS...

OF COURSE, COMMISSIONER.

YOU KNOW WHAT'S *WEIRD?* DOESN'T IT SAY SOMEWHERE IN THE BIBLE ABOUT RICH MEN NOT BEING ABLE TO GET INTO HEAVEN?

SOME-THING LIKE THAT, YES.

SO WHY DOES THE REVEREND HAVE A *SOLID GOLD* CRUCIFIX IN HIS *TWO MILLION-DOLLAR* PENTHOUSE APARTMENT?

WHERE DOES HE THINK THAT'LL GET HIM WHEN THE *END TIMES* COME?

I DON'T KNOW. MAYBE THERE'S A *COVER CHARGE* FOR THE *WHITES-ONLY* SECTION OF HEAVEN.

SO YOU *HAVE* WATCHED THIS GUY'S SHOW.

WHAT, DRIVER? I SAID I WAS FOLLOWING MY GUT ON THIS THING.

I DIDN'T SAY A WORD.

LIKE YOU HAVE TO. I SAW THAT LOOK WHEN I PULLED OUT THE NECKLACE.

OKAY, FINE. I'D JUST LIKE TO KNOW WHERE THIS GUT FEELING CAME FROM, THAT'S ALL.

I SEE AN EXPENSIVE PIECE OF JEWELRY ON THE CARPET BY AN OPEN SAFE AT THE SCENE OF A ROBBERY/HOMICIDE, MY FIRST THOUGHT ISN'T THAT IT'S PLANTED.

MINE, EITHER. IT WAS MY SECOND THOUGHT.

BUT WHY?

I DON'T KNOW, I MEAN, LOOK AT THE GUY'S APARTMENT. IT'S LOADED WITH STUFF WORTH JUST AS MUCH AS THIS PIECE. SO WHY IS THIS IN A SAFE BUT THE REST IS ON DISPLAY?

MAYBE BECAUSE THAT NECKLACE IS SMALL ENOUGH TO WALK AWAY WITH?

HEY, GUYS, YOUR VIC WAS THAT TV BORN-AGAIN GUY, RIGHT?

HEY, ROMY...YEAH, WHY?

EARLY EDITION OF THE GAZETTE.

Grief: Iraqi man carries son killed in

REVEREND PRESSMAN MURDERED!

CATWOMAN SUSPECTED

An Exclusive by SIMON LIPPM

The late Reverend Preston speaking at Cathedral Square last June

HELLO, SIMON...

...DON'T YOU THINK THE LEAST YOU COULD'VE DONE WAS CALL US FOR A COMMENT?

I THOUGHT WE WERE *FRIENDS,* AFTER ALL.

LOOK, I *KNOW,* OKAY? BUT MY NEW EDITOR'S AN *ASS.*

HE SAW AKINS' LITTLE *CONFERENCE* LAST NIGHT AND KNEW HE WAS SITTING ON *SOMETHING,* SO WHEN THIS DROPPED INTO MY LAP, HE MADE ME RUN WITH IT.

LIKE YOU GUYS WOULD'VE GIVEN ANYTHING MORE THAN A *NO COMMENT* ANYWAY.

BUT IT WOULD'VE BEEN NICE TO KNOW AHEAD OF TIME THAT OUR ⚡#*% WAS GOING TO GET PUT ALL OVER THE STREET.

YOU GOT *YOUR* BOSSES, AND I GOT *MINE,* JOSIE. WE DON'T PICK THEM.

THINK YOUR GIRL MESSED UP AGAIN, DAD.

MY PARTNER, WHO I LIKE A *LOT*, REALLY...HE'S STARTING TO *CATCH ON*, I THINK, LIKE THE LAST ONE DID.

MAYBE I JUST GET TOO COCKY ABOUT IT. I DON'T KNOW.

BUT I DON'T KNOW WHAT TO *DO* NOW.

I FEEL LIKE A BOTTLE THAT A *GENIE* IS TRYING TO BUST LOOSE FROM OR SOMETHING, AND ONCE IT ESCAPES, THERE'LL BE NO TURNING BACK, WILL THERE?

THEY'LL ALL THINK I'M LIKE *THEM*...THE *OTHER* FREAKS OF GOTHAM.

WHAT CAN I DO? I CAN'T **HELP** IT.

I JUST **LOOK** AT THINGS, AND I KNOW WHERE THEY COME FROM, OR THEY **CALL OUT** TO ME.

LIKE REMEMBER THAT **PREACHER** ON TV WHO USED TO DRIVE YOU UP THE WALL, DAD?

WELL, MAYBE HE'S OVER THERE WITH YOU NOW, THOUGH I **DOUBT IT,** REALLY. HE'S PROBABLY AT A MUCH **WARMER** ADDRESS...

ANYWAY, HE GOT **KILLED,** AND WE'RE WALKING THROUGH THE SCENE, AND THIS NECKLACE ON THE FLOOR JUST **TELLS ME** IT'S FROM SOMEWHERE ELSE.

I DON'T KNOW WHERE, BUT IT WASN'T FROM THE **SAFE** IN THAT ROOM. SO, WHAT AM I SUPPOSED TO **DO?** IGNORE THAT?

THIS THING, WHATEVER IT IS, IT HELPS ME BE A BETTER COP, DAD...

BUT IF THE REST OF THEM FIND OUT, IT'S GOING TO RIP ME APART, TOO.

I **HATE** TO INTERRUPT THIS HEART-WARMING LITTLE SCENE, BUT...

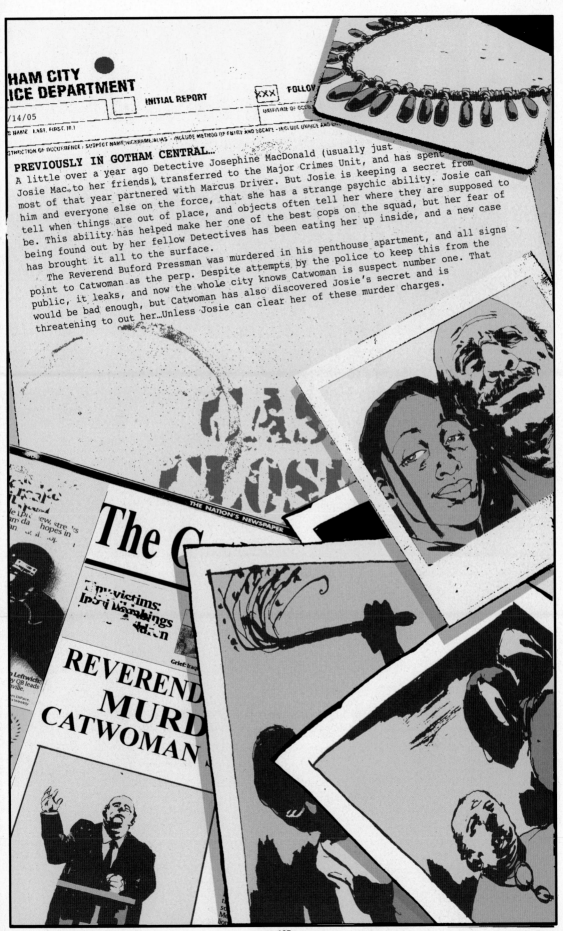

PREVIOUSLY IN GOTHAM CENTRAL...

A little over a year ago Detective Josephine MacDonald (usually just Josie Mac to her friends), transferred to the Major Crimes Unit, and has spent most of that year partnered with Marcus Driver. But Josie is keeping a secret from him and everyone else on the force, that she has a strange psychic ability. Josie can tell when things are out of place, and objects often tell her where they are supposed to be. This ability has helped make her one of the best cops on the squad, but her fear of being found out by her fellow Detectives has been eating her up inside, and a new case has brought it all to the surface.

The Reverend Buford Pressman was murdered in his penthouse apartment, and all signs point to Catwoman as the perp. Despite attempts by the police to keep this from the public, it leaks, and now the whole city knows Catwoman is suspect number one. That would be bad enough, but Catwoman has also discovered Josie's secret and is threatening to out her...Unless Josie can clear her of these murder charges.

...STUPIDEST THING I *EVER* HEARD, SWEAR TO GOD.

IT'S *TRUE*, SARGE, A DOG'S SALIVA HAS *ANTISEPTIC* PROPERTIES. THEY LICK THEIR WOUNDS TO HELP *HEAL* THEM, IT'S A SCIENTIFIC FACT.

RIGHT, SO NEXT TIME I CUT MYSELF SHAVIN', I'LL JUST GET YOUR LITTLE MUTT TO LICK MY FACE.

EXACTLY.

YOU SPEND ENTIRELY TOO MUCH TIME ON THAT *INTERNET*, CROWE.

HEY, JOSIE. YOU OKAY?

FINE...JUST GOT A LITTLE *HELD UP*. ANY NEWS ON OUR CASE?

A BIT. M.E. SAYS THE SCRATCHES ON OUR VIC'S FACE WERE THERE FOR AT LEAST AN HOUR BEFORE HE GOT SHOT.

SO, UNLESS HE *FAINTED* WHEN SHE SCRATCHED HIM AND SHE WAITED AROUND TO DO THE DEED...

...IT LOOKS LIKE YOUR *GUT* WAS RIGHT...

...AS *USUAL*.

--LOOKIN' FOR DIRT ON PRESSMAN. HE HAD SOME SCUMMY *LAND DEAL* ABOUT TO GO THROUGH IN THE EAST END.

GONNA PUT A LOT OF PEOPLE WHO GOT NOWHERE ELSE TO *GO* OUT ON THE STREET. SHE WAS TRYING TO SHUT IT *DOWN*...

...AN' AS YOU CAN SEE, SHE HIT THE *JACKPOT.*

YEAH... THIS IS...

...OH, MAN, *EWWW.*

I KNOW. AND THIS IS JUST A FEW OF THE STILLS.

WAS SOME KINDA *HARD-DRIVE* IN THAT SAFE, FILLED WITH MORE OF THE SAME, EXCEPT IN MOVING PICTURES. MO-PEGS OR WHATEVER.

MPEGS.

YEAH, THAT. HAD MY TECH GUY PRINT THESE OUT FOR YOU. BUT SHE WANTS TO HOLD ONTO THE HARD-DRIVE UNTIL THIS ALL BLOWS OVER, JUST IN CASE.

SO, LET ME SEE IF I'VE GOT THIS STRAIGHT.

SHE STEALS *THIS* FROM PRESSMAN'S SAFE AND TELLS HIM SHE'LL GO *PUBLIC* WITH HIS DIRTY SECRETS UNLESS HE PULLS THE PLUG ON SOME CROOKED *REAL ESTATE* DEAL IN THE EAST END?

THAT'S ABOUT THE SIZE OF IT.

THESE PICTURES, IF THEY'RE **REAL**...THAT WOULD'VE BEEN THE **END** OF PRESSMAN AND HIS WHOLE *"OUR SAVIOR HOUR"* FRANCHISE.

YEAH, IT WOULD'VE... SO, I'M THINKING PRESSMAN WOULD'VE CAVED.

UNLESS HE WAS CRAZY... AND THERE'S SOME CRAZY $#% HERE, FOR SURE.

YOU SAID A MOUTHFUL, TOOTS.

TOOTS?

SORRY, I MEANT **DETECTIVE** TOOTS.

SO... WHAT'RE YOU THINKIN'?

I'M WONDERING WHO THIS WOMAN HERE IN THE ZIPPER **MASK** IS, FOR ONE...

AN' YOU'RE WONDERIN' WHO THE HELL THAT **CAMERAMAN** IS, RIGHT?

GIVE THE MAN A PRIZE.

JESUS...WHY IS IT ALWAYS THE ZEALOTS WHO'RE HIDING THE REAL PERVY $#%?

IT'S **NOT**. THIS GUY JUST **HAPPENS** TO BE A PERV. DOESN'T CONDEMN ALL PREACHERS.

MAYBE NOT TO YOU.

SO SOME **SNITCH** OF YOURS JUST **HAPPENED** TO COME ACROSS THESE? AND SWEARS **THIS** IS WHAT WAS IN THE REVEREND'S SAFE?

LET'S NOT LOOK A GIFT HORSE IN THE MOUTH, DRIVER, OKAY?

WHAT IS THAT **FROM?** THE **TROJAN WAR,** RIGHT?

AND SEE, IF THEY **HAD** LOOKED THAT HORSE IN THE MOUTH, THEY MIGHT NOT'VE DRAGGED A WHOLE **ARMY** INSIDE TO RAPE AND PILLAGE THEIR CITY.

SO REALLY THAT SAYING **SHOULD** BE, **ALWAYS** LOOK A GIFT HORSE IN THE MOUTH.

FINE, **WHATEVER.**

IN ANY CASE...WE'VE NOW GOT A FEW OTHER ANGLES TO LOOK AT ON THIS MURDER.

OKAY. BUT WHAT DOES THIS **MEAN,** REALLY?

YOUR **SOURCE** SAYS CATWOMAN WAS GOING TO **BLACKMAIL** THE REV WITH HIS DIRTY LITTLE SECRET, AND HE'D PROBABLY HAVE GONE ALONG WITH IT...SO, WHO'RE WE **LOOKING** FOR?

SOMEONE WHO DIDN'T WANT THE REV TO GIVE IN TO BLACKMAIL?

OR SOMEONE WHO FOUND OUT ABOUT HIS BONDAGE FETISH AND JUST LOST IT?

YEAH, I'M THINKING MRS. PRESSMAN EITHER ALREADY **KNEW** ABOUT THIS OR WOULDN'T REALLY **CARE**, WAY SHE WAS ACTING.

THAT **SECRETARY** OF HIS, THOUGH, SHE WAS WOUND PRETTY TIGHT. I COULD SEE HER FLIPPING OUT IF SHE FOUND OUT ABOUT HER BOSS'S PRIVATE LIFE.

TRUE...BUT I DON'T SEE HER AS CALCULATING ENOUGH TO **COVER IT UP**, THEN COME BACK AND DISCOVER THE **BODY**.

PLUS, THE **LUDS** FROM THE MINISTRY OFFICE SHOW THAT SHE **DID** CALL PRESSMAN'S--

HEY--

WAIT... LET ME SEE...

...MOTHER-#%€*#...

WHAT?

PRESSMAN'S **CELL PHONE.** IT WASN'T WITH HIS EFFECTS AND IT'S NOT LISTED AT THE **CRIME SCENE,** EITHER.

SOMEONE JUST GOT **VERY** STUPID.

GET THE LUDS FOR PRESSMAN'S CELL. HE MUST'VE CALLED SOMEONE AFTER CATWOMAN LEFT.

WHERE ARE **YOU** GOING?

TO HAVE ANOTHER TALK WITH OUR **FRIEND** FROM THE **GAZETTE.**

GOT A MINUTE?

ARE YOU *KIDDING* ME? YOU THINK YOU CAN SWEET-TALK ME IF YOU COME BY *YOURSELF*, JOSIE?

YOU THINK MY ETHICS ARE SO CHEAP THAT A PRETTY SMILE WILL SWAY ME?

NO, SIMON, I *DON'T.*

AND I DON'T WANT YOU TO TELL ME WHO YOUR SOURCE IS ANYMORE.

THEN WHAT ARE YOU DOING HERE?

I CAME TO OFFER YOU A *DEAL.*

RIIIGHT.

SERIOUSLY. I'M GOING TO GIVE YOU THE SCOOP OF YOUR CAREER.

BUT I'M ALSO GOING TO APPEAL TO YOUR *FINER* INSTINCTS, TOO. BECAUSE I STILL BELIEVE YOU'RE ONE OF THE GOOD ONES, SIMON.

YOU SEE THAT? LOOKED RIGHT OVER HERE AND *STILL* DIDN'T MAKE US.

DOESN'T KNOW WHAT TO LOOK FOR. HE'S *NEW* AT THIS, REMEMBER?

HOW COULD I *FORGET*?

I MEAN, THIS MCMILLAN GUY ACTUALLY THOUGHT WE WOULDN'T CHECK WHO THE REV'S LAST CALLS WERE TO. TALK ABOUT AMATEUR HOUR.

IT'S NOT *THAT* DUMB, REALLY. IT'S GOTHAM, AFTER ALL, AND IT LOOKS LIKE CATWOMAN DID IT.

MOST COPS WOULDN'T'VE LOOKED ANY HARDER FROM THAT POINT.

SO, YOU ACTUALLY *BELIEVE* IN GOD AND THE BIBLE AND ALL THAT?

YEAH, MOSTLY. GOD, AT LEAST...NOT SO SURE ABOUT THE *BIBLE* SOMETIMES.

YOU *DON'T?*

NAH...GOD'S LIKE SANTA CLAUS FOR ADULTS, FAR AS I'M CONCERNED.

OH, AND NOW YOU'RE TELLING ME YOU DON'T BELIEVE IN *SANTA,* EITHER?

CUFFS
CLAWS

OH, LOOK AT *THIS.* SOOO PREDICTABLE.

PEOPLE ARE SUCH A DISAPPOINTMENT MOST OF THE TIME.

DO WE WAIT OR DO WE FOLLOW HIM INSIDE?

YOU REALLY WANT TO GO WALKING INTO A SEX CLUB WAVING BADGES?

SURE, COULD BE FUN. GOTTA BRING McMILLAN IN ANYWAY, MAYBE HE'S MEETING WITH THE CHICK FROM THE VIDEOS.

HELL, I'M GAME IF YOU ARE...

--WASN'T LIKE I SET OUT TO KILL HIM. I MEAN, I *LOVED* BUFORD. HE WAS LIKE MY BEST FRIEND OR SOMETHING...

BUT HE WAS JUST CRAZY THAT NIGHT. HE CALLED ME AND TOLD ME WHAT HAD HAPPENED, THAT CATWOMAN HAD STOLEN HIS PRIVATE VIDEOS.

BUT WHEN I GOT OVER THERE, I MEAN, I WAS GOING TO TRY AND CALM HIM DOWN...AND THEN HE PULLS OUT THIS GUN.

SAYS HE'S GOING TO KILL US *BOTH*. I MEAN, HE WAS BLAMING *ME* FOR THE WHOLE THING.

SAID IF HE'D NEVER MET ME, HE'D NEVER HAVE GIVEN IN TO HIS *DEMONS* OR WHATEVER.

I DIDN'T *MEAN* TO SHOOT HIM, I JUST--IT WAS ME OR HIM, Y'KNOW? *SELF-DEFENSE*.

BUT BUFORD, HE JUST--HE WAS *ALREADY* ON THE EDGE. *BEFORE* THE WHOLE THING WITH CATWOMAN. HE WAS ALREADY GOING A LITTLE WACKO.

KEEPING THAT SECRET... WHAT HE WAS REALLY INTO...

...HE COULDN'T HANDLE THAT KIND OF *WEIGHT*.

JUST WASN'T *BUILT* FOR IT.

SO, IT'S DONE?

JUMPY, DETECTIVE JOSIE MAC. AND HERE I THOUGHT YOU WERE STEADY AS A ROCK.

SO, IS IT DONE? AM I CLEAR OF THIS MESS?

JESUS!

WHAT THE *HELL* DO YOU THINK YOU'RE DOING?

YEAH, YOU'RE CLEAR, OF THE *MURDER* AT LEAST. I DON'T CARE ABOUT THE B. AND E., BUT SOMEONE MIGHT.

SO, MCMILLAN GAVE IT ALL UP, THEN?

THE END

KEYSTONE KOPS

Written by
GREG RUCKA

Pencils by
STEFANO GAUDIANO

Inks by
GAUDIANO *(Part One & Two),* **KANO** *(Part Three),* **AND GARY AMARO** *(Part Four)*

Colors by
LEE LOUGHRIDGE

Letters by
CLEM ROBINS

‹...YOU'RE GONNA **HELP** ME WITH THE **HOMEWORK**, RIGHT?›

‹...MY PARENTS WON'T EVEN LET ME **WATCH** IT, THEY SAY IT'S **TOO VIOLENT**--›

‹--BUT I **DIDN'T**, BUT MS. DOMINGUEZ, SHE SAID I **DID**, SO NOW I GOTTA WRITE THE **WHOLE** THING **AGAIN**!›

IT WAS **SICK** THE WAY YOU **FACED** JESUS, MAN! TOTALLY PUT HIM **DOWN**!

DON'T **SAY** THAT, MAN. I WASN'T LOOKING FOR ANY **TROUBLE**.

‹MIGUEL! WAIT UP!›

‹C'MON, ANNA, **HURRY**, WOULD YOU?›

‹MAMA SAYS YOU'RE SUPPOSED TO **WAIT** FOR ME, SHE SAYS YOU'RE SUPPOSED TO WALK **WITH** ME ALL THE WAY **HOME**.›

I'LL CATCH YOU LATER, MIGUEL.

SEE YOU TOMORROW.

‹I **AM** WALKING WITH YOU.›

‹YOUR **LEGS** ARE **TOO** LONG! SLOW DOWN!›

‹YOU GOTTA KEEP UP!›

‹WE **HURRY**, WE CAN WATCH SOME CARTOONS BEFORE MAMA GETS HOME--›

‹YOU BETTER HOPE YOUR MAMA'S *WAITING,* MIGUEL, 'CAUSE *YOU'RE* GONNA *NEED* HER.›

‹JESUS... C'MON, MAN--›

‹SHUT *UP!* YOU TALK LIKE *THAT,* LIKE WE'RE *FRIENDS,* YOU LITTLE *PUNK?*›

‹WE'RE *NOT* FRIENDS, FRIENDS DON'T *RAT* YOU *OUT,* DON'T GET YOU *EXPELLED!*›

‹IT'S NOT *MY* FAULT YOU HAD A *KNIFE* AT *SCHOOL!*›

‹IT'S NOT *MY* FAULT YOU *PULLED* IT OR THAT THEY *TOOK* IT FROM YOU!›

‹GOOD THING I GOT ME A *NEW* ONE, THEN, HUH?›

‹WHICH EYE SHOULD I *TAKE,* YOU PIECE OF ¢*%$#?›

NGHH!

‹ANNA! RUN TO *MONTOYA'S!* STAY THERE!›

RUN!

MIGUEL!

...TWENTY-THREE CENTS BACK.

THANKS, MISTER MONTOYA.

I DUNNO, ANDY, I THINK IT'S *ACID REFLUX* OR SOMETHING.

YOU SHOULD HAVE IT CHECKED *OUT,* DON. THAT'S A *SERIOUS* MEDICAL--

HELP! SOMEONE *PLEASE* HELP--

--IT'S JESUS, HE'S TRYING TO *KILL* MY *BROTHER*--

EASY, SWEET-HEART--

--HE'S TRYING TO KILL MIGUEL!

PLEASE, YOU'VE GOT TO *HELP* HIM!

WHICH WAY, HON?

IT WAS AROUND THE CORNER, THEY WENT AROUND THE CORNER--

STAY WITH MISTER MONTOYA.

Keystone Kops Part One

DON! GONNA NEED SOME **HELP** HERE!

⟨I'M OFFICER **KELLY**, OKAY? ANDREW KELLY, I'M GONNA **HELP** YOU, BUT YOU GOTTA STAY **CALM**.⟩

⟨PLEASE...IT **HURTS**...⟩

OKAY, MY **SPANISH** ISN'T THAT **GOOD**. YOU UNDERSTAND ME IF I SPEAK **ENGLISH**?

HE **DOES**, WE **BOTH** DO.

OKAY, I'M GONNA TRY TO PULL YOU **FREE**, ALL RIGHT?

JESUS CHRIST.

TOOK YOUR **TIME** THERE, DON.

YEAH, WELL, I'M **HERE** NOW, PARTNER...

...TELL ME WHAT YOU **NEED**.

CATCH THIS **KID**, OKAY?

GOTCHA.

HNNN!

GHAHHHH!!

TAKE HIM!

UFF

THIS KID NEEDS A *DOCTOR* BAD, ANDY.

HNNNHHN HNNNGG

GET HIM *UPSTAIRS*, I'LL GET THE *OTHER* ONE.

FROM THE *CUT* ON YOUR *FACE*, I'M GUESSING YOU'RE MIGUEL?

...YEAH...

I MET YOUR *SISTER*. SHE'S GONNA BE *HAPPY* YOU'RE OKAY.

YEAH. SHE'S KINDA A *PAIN*, THOUGH.

YEAH, I FEEL THE *SAME* WAY ABOUT *MY* KID SISTER.

OKAY, HERE'S WHAT WE'RE GONNA DO...

...YOU'RE GONNA *JUMP* TO ME, OKAY?

THAT WAY *NEITHER* OF US *STEPS* IN THIS *STUFF,* WHATEVER IT IS.

SAY *WHAT?*

YOU'RE GONNA *JUMP,* MIGUEL.

I'M GONNA *CATCH* YOU.

C'MON, *NEITHER* OF US WANTS TO *WALK* IN THIS STUFF, RIGHT?

I'LL KEEP YOU *SAFE.*

MY MAMA, SHE SAYS **COPS,** THEY JUST WANT **MONEY.**

YEAH. I'M **NOT** ONE OF **THOSE.**

YOU CAN **TRUST** ME. COME ON...

...YOU CAN **DO** IT...

KSSSH

...BUT THE **BEST** THING ABOUT GETTING BACK ON **DAYS**...

...I GET TO SPEND TIME WITH MY **KIDS** AGAIN.

NOT TO MENTION DORE.

THAT, **TOO.**

WE'VE GOT **TROUBLE**...

...A **UNIT** WALKED INTO SOME **FREAK'S** HIDEOUT UP ON VAN BUREN AT A HUNDRED AND FIFTY-SIXTH.

ONE OF THE OFFICERS GOT **FRIED,** HE'S ON HIS WAY TO ST. LUKE'S.

DEL ARRAZIO, BARTLETT, IT'S **YOURS.**

WE GOT **NAMES** ON THE **UNIT?**

THEY'RE OUT OF THE NORTHERN, OFFICERS PEAK AND KELLY.

KELLY'S THE ONE GOT **BURNED.**

THEY DON'T THINK HE'S GONNA **MAKE** IT.

CAPTAIN, LET **ME** TAKE IT.

WHY SHOULD I DO THAT, RENEE?

I KNOW HIM.

WE CAME THROUGH NO MAN'S LAND TOGETHER.

NO. SERGEANT, GET *UP* THERE AND LET ME KNOW WHAT YOU FIND.

WILL DO, CAPTAIN.

LET ME **HAVE** IT.

YOU HAVE A **REASON** TO THINK SERGEANT DEL ARRAZIO CAN'T **HANDLE** IT, DETECTIVE, I'D BE **INTERESTED** IN HEARING IT.

HE **DOESN'T** KNOW HIM.

ASIDE FROM THE FACT THAT DEL ARRAZIO WAS **HERE** DURING N.M.L., IT WOULD SEEM TO ME **NOT** KNOWING OFFICER KELLY IS A **BONUS** IN THIS SITUATION.

THAT'S **NOT** THE THING, CAPTAIN.

IT'S...THAT'S **MY** OLD **NEIGHBORHOOD**, KELLY...

...I GOT HIM **STARTED** ON THE **JOB** AFTER N.M.L....

...I WAS HIS **RABBI**, Y'KNOW?

PLEASE, MAGGIE...

...I'VE **NEVER** ASKED YOU FOR **ANYTHING** BEFORE...

ALL RIGHT.

BUT **ALLEN** IS THE **PRIMARY**.

YOU **HEAR** ME? I SAID **ALLEN** IS THE PRIMARY!

I'LL KEEP YOU **POSTED**.

...THAT'S WHEN I GET DOWN TO THE *BASEMENT.* SWEAR TO *GOD,* IT'S LIKE SOMETHING OUT OF A *JOKER* PLOT, THERE'RE *TEST TUBES* AND ALL THAT #5¢*.

JOKER'S *STILL* IN *ARKHAM.*

I'M SAYING IT WAS *NUTS,* DETECTIVE, THAT'S *ALL* I'M *SAYING.*

THE *FIRST* KID, WE GET HIM OUT--HE'S THE ONE THAT HAD THE *KNIFE*--I BRING HIM UP, CALL FOR AN *AMBO.* START BACK *IN...*

...RUN INTO *THAT* ONE COMING UP THE STAIRS, SCREAMING ABOUT ANDY, HOW HE'S *BURNING* ALIVE.

THAT'S *IT.*

ANY WORD ON *ANDY?*

HE'S AT *ST. LUKE'S,* THAT'S ALL WE KNOW.

I'D LIKE TO HEAD OVER THERE.

YEAH, GO *AHEAD.*

OH, FOR %5¢*'S SAKE.

VINCENT!

YOU TALKED HER *INTO* IT?

SHE GAVE IT TO *ME,* YEAH.

MEANING SHE GAVE IT TO CRIS.

YOU'VE GOT *NO* DISTANCE ON THIS CASE, RENEE, YOU KNOW THAT.

LIKE *YOU* GOT *NO* DISTANCE WHEN YOU'RE WORKING ANYTHING WITH *INZERILLO* IN ITS *NAME.*

BUT I'VE *NEVER* DOUBTED YOU DID THE JOB *RIGHT* WHEN IT WAS ALL SAID AND *DONE.*

YOU WANT US TO INTERVIEW THE *WITNESSES* OR HEAD OVER TO THE *HOSPITAL?*

SEE WHAT YOU CAN GET FROM THE *WITNESSES.*

START WITH THE *GUY* WITH THE *MUSTACHE* AND THE *APRON...*

...HE KNOWS *EVERYBODY* IN THE *NEIGHBORHOOD.*

YEAH? HOW DO YOU KNOW *THAT?*

TRUST ME, I *KNOW...*

...HE'S MY *DAD.*

MAYBE YOU SHOULD TAKE THIS OPPORTUNITY TO *REBUILD* SOME *BRIDGES*, RENEE.

THEY *DISOWNED ME*, REMEMBER?

UNLESS IT'S TO *TELL* HIM I'M SUDDENLY *STRAIGHT*...

...THAT SON OF A BITCH DOESN'T WANT TO HEAR *ANYTHING* I HAVE TO *SAY*.

IT'S **MIGUEL**, RIGHT?

I DON'T KNOW IF YOU **REMEMBER** ME, I'M **RENEE**.

YOU'RE MISTER **MONTOYA'S DAUGHTER**. YOU'RE THE **COP**.

YEAH, I'M A **DETECTIVE**. THIS IS MY **PARTNER**, HIS NAME IS **CRIS**.

CAN YOU TELL ME WHAT **HAPPENED** IN THERE, MIGUEL?

JESUS...JESUS **CHASED** ME, HE HAD A **KNIFE**. I RAN INTO THE BUILDING, THEN DOWN THE **STAIRS**...

...THE **BASEMENT**, IT LOOKED LIKE THE **CHEMISTRY** LAB AT **SCHOOL**, THERE WERE ALL THESE **BEAKERS** AND **TEST TUBES**...

...I--I **KNOCKED** SOME **OVER** AND THEY **BROKE** AND IT **CAUGHT** JESUS, IT MADE HIM GET **STUCK**.

THE **COP** CAME, HE GOT US **OUT**...

⟨...IT'S **MY FAULT**!⟩

⟨THE **COP** PICKED ME **UP**, BUT I **KNOCKED** THE **TUBE** OVER AND IT **BROKE** AND IT MADE THE **FIRE**!⟩

⟨**TELL** ME ABOUT THE **FIRE**, MIGUEL.⟩

⟨IT WAS...IT **WASN'T** LIKE **REAL** FIRE, RENEE! IT **BURNED**, BUT IT WASN'T **HOT**...⟩

⟨...IT'S **MY** FAULT...⟩

⟨...HE WAS TRYING TO **SAVE** ME...⟩

146

NOT YOUR **AVERAGE** WEENIE ROAST.

TELL ME ABOUT IT.

INSPECTOR LANNING, G.C.F.D.

M.C.U. RENEE MONTOYA, THIS IS CRISPUS ALLEN.

WHAT CAN YOU **TELL** US?

JUST ABOUT **SQUAT,** HONESTLY. NEVER SEEN **ANYTHING** LIKE THIS.

LOOKS LIKE AN **AMMONIA** FIRE IN A LOT OF WAYS, BUT I'M NOT SEEING ANY OF THE **TRADITIONAL** HEAT SCARRING...

...**FIRE** CLIMBS, IT WANTS TO GO **UP,** YOU KNOW? BUT THESE **WALLS** ARE CLEAN, IT'S LIKE IT HUGGED THE **FLOOR** AND NEVER **ROSE.**

NOT EVEN **SMOKE** STAINS HERE.

MIGUEL-- THE KID OUTSIDE-- SAYS IT **BURNT** BUT THERE WAS NO **HEAT.**

KID'S A *MORON,* IT'S *NOT* POSSIBLE.

HE'S A *GOOD* KID, I KNOW HIS *MOTHER.*

YOU CAN SPEND CHRISTMAS WITH HIS FAMILY ALL I CARE, HE *STILL* DOESN'T KNOW WHAT HE'S *TALKING* ABOUT.

FIRE GENERATES *HEAT,* THAT'S THE WAY--

HEY...

COULD YOU MAYBE *SHINE* THAT *LIGHT* AT MY FEET INSTEAD OF AT MY *FACE,* LANNING?

YOU GOT *SOME-THING?*

YEAH, MAYBE...

...LOOKS LIKE THE *PERIODIC TABLE...*

THE *WHAT?*

THE *ELEMENTS,* YOU KNOW, IT WAS ON THE WALL OF YOUR CHEMISTRY CLASS IN HIGH SCHOOL?

I *CUT* CHEM.

...WHO THE *HELL* IS ALBERT DESMOND?

LET'S FIND *OUT.*

STACY? RENEE. BRING UP THE NVAC, RUN THE NAME *ALBERT DESMOND,* WOULD YOU?

THAT'S *WRONG,* THOSE ELEMENTS *DON'T* EXIST.

TECHNICALLY THEY *DO.* THEY JUST HAVEN'T BEEN *DISCOVERED* YET.

LOOKS LIKE *THIS* GUY THINKS HE'S A *GENIUS.*

HE *DOES.*

ALBERT DESMOND, A.K.A. *DOCTOR ALCHEMY.*

HE'S CURRENTLY A *GUEST* OF THE *STATE* AT IRON HEIGHTS, OUTSIDE OF KEYSTONE CITY...

...HE'S A MEMBER OF THE *ROGUES.*

GOT[...]
PO[...]

DATE

WITNESS

RECONST[...]

SCARS, MARKS, M.O. ETC.

[...]king
[...]ation

[...]om ANNA NAVARRO, claiming her older
[...]OLD was being assaulted by a group of youths, led by one JESUS
"STICKY" ACOSTA (JOI-47890-900). Officers ANDREW KELLY (Badge#45892) and
DONALD PEAK (Badge#42061) responded on foot, arriving at 98992 Van Buren
Avenue at approximately 1555 hours, today's date.

Upon effecting entry to the building, Officer Kelly encountered both subject
Miguel Navarro and suspect Acosta in the basement. later investigation of
the site concluded that the basement had been used prior as a laboratory for
DOCTOR ALBERT DESMOND, aka DOCTOR ALCHEMY (NVAC:K-F-76332/B, attached) and
since abandoned.

Ascertaining that Navarro and Acosta were trapped in the hazardous environment,
Officers Kelly and Peak succeeded in freeing Acosta, who Peak then removed
from the scene for medical treatment, leaving Officer Kelly to rescue Navarro.
During this rescue attempt, a fire of unknown origin and cause erupted,
consuming Kelly while he protected Navarro from the flames.

At this time, Officer Kelly remains at Saint Luke's Hospital receiving
treatment for burns and exposure to chemicals of unknown origin.

Submitted this [...]
Detective 2nd [...]

Renee

PAGE

SUPERVISOR APPROVAL

FOLLOWUP-CONTINUATION [...]

ALBERT DESMOND a/k/a
DOCTOR ALCHEMY

Keystone Kops Part Two

HHNNHNNRAAA

SHARON?

SHARON!

OH, MY GOD, DON--

AAAARRHHGNNN

--SOMETHING'S *HAPPENING* TO HIM, SOMETHING'S HAPPENING TO ANDY!

GNNGHHNNN

HE KEEPS *SCREAMING*, DON.

HE *KEEPS* SCREAMING...

NNHHAAAHAAANN

HE DOESN'T *STOP*...

NNH HNNHN HNN

WE NEED TO **CHASE** THIS **DOCTOR ALCHEMY** THING DOWN.

LET'S HEAD **BACK,** THEN, DO IT FROM **CENTRAL.**

YEAH, THAT'S... ...DAMMIT...

CAN YOU GET A LIFT BACK WITH VIN AND JOE?

I NEED TO **DO** SOMETHING ELSE **FIRST.**

YOU **SURE** YOU WANT TO DO IT **ALONE?**

I THINK I'LL BE ALL RIGHT, THANKS.

YOU'RE A GOOD PARTNER, CRIS.

WE'RE ABOUT TO **CLOSE,** SO PLEASE MAKE IT FAST.

DING DING

HEY, PAPI.

⟨I ALREADY SPOKE TO YOUR *FELLOW* DETECTIVES.⟩

⟨I DON'T KNOW *WHAT* I CAN TELL *YOU* THAT I DIDN'T ALREADY TELL *THEM*.⟩

⟨IF YOU'LL *EXCUSE* ME, I HAVE TO CLOSE UP NOW.⟩

⟨I HAVE TO GET HOME FOR *DINNER*.⟩

⟨SURE.⟩

⟨SORRY TO HAVE **BOTHERED** YOU.⟩

⟨HEY.⟩

⟨ARE YOU...⟩

⟨...ARE YOU **STILL** SEEING THAT **GIRL**?⟩

⟨HER NAME'S **DARIA.**⟩

⟨WE'VE BEEN LIVING **TOGETHER** FOR ALMOST A **YEAR** NOW.⟩

⟨OH.⟩

DING DING

--NO, MAN, IT'S **CHANGING** HIM **SOMEHOW**, SOME **MAD SCIENTIST** $#%¢.

WHATEVER KELLY WALKED **INTO**, DEFINITELY A **FREAK** THING.

MAYBE WE CAN START **TAKING** THOSE PEST BASTARDS **DOWN** PERMANENT-LIKE NOW THAT WE GOT THE **BAT** OUT OF OUR--

HEY, MONTOYA!

DETECTIVE, HOLD UP A SEC!

MAKE IT FAST, DOGNAVICH.

YOU'RE WORKING THE VAN BUREN **CALL**? THE ONE THAT **BURNED** KELLY?

I AM.

YOU **FIND** THE **FREAK** WHO DID IT, YOU LET US **KNOW**, DETECTIVE, OKAY?

I MEAN...MAYBE WE **PATROL** SLOBS DON'T HAVE A LOT OF **LOVE** FOR YOU **THINKERS** IN THE M.C.U., BUT KELLY'S A **GOOD** POLICE...

...YOU GOT **HALF** THE COPS IN THE WESTERN **BREAKING** HEADS TONIGHT, TRYING TO FIND THE S.O.B. WHO HURT OUR **BOY.**

TRYING TO **FIND** THE MOTHER*¢%#* BEFORE **YOU** GUYS DO.

--YOU HAVE **ONE** OF THEM CALL ME, THEY GET THE MESSAGE, OKAY?

YEAH, DETECTIVE CRISPUS ALLEN, G.C.P.D., MAJOR CRIMES UNIT...

TAKE A **LOOK.**

WHAT IS IT?

MY MAN MARCUS HERE PUT TOGETHER A LITTLE **DOSSIER** ON DOCTOR ALCHEMY...

...SEEMS OFFICER ANDREW KELLY HAS A **LOT** OF **FRIENDS.**

HE DOES.

CRIS? YOU GOT ANYTHING?

KEYSTONE P.D. IS CHECKING THAT ALBERT DESMOND IS **STILL** INCARCERATED AT IRON HEIGHTS.

GOT A LINE ON A DETECTIVE OUT THERE, NAME OF CHYRE, WAITING FOR A CALL **BACK.**

THERE **ANY** PHYSICAL EVIDENCE THAT **TIES** THIS WHACKO TO THE SCENE?

OTHER THAN THAT **PERIODIC TABLE?** NOTHING YET.

WAY THE **LAB** WORKS, IT'LL BE ANOTHER FEW **DAYS,** AND THAT'S IF WE'RE **REALLY** LUCKY, PARTNER.

NOT LIKELY.

JOELY, YOU HEAR FROM THE **HOSPITAL**?

YEAH. **NOT** GOOD, RENEE.

HE'S IN A **LOT** OF **PAIN**. SOMETHING'S **HAPPENING** TO HIS **BODY**.

THERE'S SOME **SPECIALIST** FROM S.T.A.R. GOTHAM TAKING A LOOK AT HIM NOW.

LIKE **THAT'LL** HELP.

BRRRTTT
BRRRTTT

M.C.U., ALLEN.

...YEAH, THAT'S RIGHT, THAT WAS ME...

...NO, IT'S **OFFICER-INVOLVED**...YES, EXACTLY...

...ALL RIGHT, THANK YOU, DETECTIVE.

KEYSTONE?

YEAH. DESMOND'S **STILL** LOCKED UP.

BEFORE HIS **LAST** GO-ROUND WITH THE **FLASH**, THOUGH, HE DISAPPEARED FOR A WHILE. MIGHT'VE BEEN WHEN HE CAME TO GOTHAM.

I THINK HE'S **OUR** GUY, RENEE.

NO QUESTION, I THINK HE'S **OUR** GUY.

...GO ON...

...IS THERE *ANY* WAY TO *REVERSE* IT?

...I SEE...

...YES, THANK YOU. KEEP ME INFORMED.

THAT ABOUT KELLY?

YEAH, WHATEVER IT IS, IT'S GETTING *WORSE.*

WHAT'S THIS?

THAT IS DOCTOR ALBERT DESMOND, CAP. *Ph.D.*s IN CHEMISTRY, BIOCHEMISTRY, MOLECULAR BIOLOGY--

--AND THE BAND PLAYS *ON*--

--CURRENTLY BEHIND *LOCK* AND *KEY* AT IRON HEIGHTS CORRECTIONAL, KEYSTONE.

HE FITS?

LIKE A *GLOVE,* CAPTAIN.

WE'RE THINKING WE NEED TO *TALK* TO HIM, AND *SOON.*

SOONER THAN YOU *THINK.*

I JUST GOT OFF WITH THE *ATTENDING* AT ST. LUKE'S.

KELLY IS *MUTATING.*

MUTATING *HOW?*

I LOOK LIKE THE *SPECIALIST* FROM S.T.A.R. LABS TO YOU, DETECTIVE ALLEN?

NO, MA'AM.

NOBODY *KNOWS.*

AND *NOBODY* KNOWS HOW TO *STOP* IT.

DESMOND *DOES.*

IT WAS HIS BOOBY TRAP. IF *ANYONE* CAN REVERSE IT, IT'LL BE DESMOND.

THAT ASSUMES HE'D *WANT* TO HELP US.

YOU THINK WE CAN *DEAL* WITH HIM?

DOUBT IT. DOUBT THERE'S *ANYTHING* WE CAN EVEN *OFFER* HIM.

WELL, YOU'RE GOING TO FIND *OUT.*

STACY!

CAPTAIN?

FIND OUT WHEN THE *FIRST* FLIGHT TO *KEYSTONE* IS IN THE MORNING...

...WE'RE GONNA NEED *TICKETS* FOR CRIS AND RENEE.

DEE, YOU HOME?

I'VE GOT TO GO TO KEYSTONE TOMORROW...

DEE?

KLK

KLK- KLK

DAMMIT.

KLK- KLK- KLK

HOLD IT--

--NHH!

166

DETECTIVE.

JESUS!

CAN'T YOU JUST SAY *HELLO* LIKE *NORMAL* PEOPLE?

DESMOND.

DON'T DEAL.

I *WON'T* ASK *HOW* YOU KNOW.

IF DESMOND CAN *SAVE* OFFICER KELLY--

HE *CAN'T.*

NO DEALS.

YOU *DIDN'T* USED TO BE SO *COLD.*

YOU *WOULD* KNOW.

KLK

THIS IS NEW. BEEN STANDING IN THE **DARK** FOR LONG?

NOT *TOO* LONG.

I *THINK* I'M *RELIEVED.*

SO JASON ORDERED TOO MUCH **SALMON** FOR THE **SPECIAL,** SO I THOUGHT I'D--

--WHOA, COWGIRL!

YOU'LL BE *BACK* TOMORROW NIGHT?

SHOULD BE.

BRING ME A *SOUVENIR,* ONE OF THOSE *FLASH* SHIRTS, SOMETHING LIKE THAT.

I'LL *TRY.*

WHAT IS IT?

I SAW MY FATHER. I WENT BY THE BODEGA, TRIED TO SAY HELLO.

HOW'D IT GO?

NOTHING'S *CHANGED.*

RENEE, DON'T DO THIS TO YOURSELF.

A YEAR AND A *HALF* AND *NOTHING'S* CHANGED, DEE.

NOTHING'S CHANGED.

EXCEPT ME.

DADDY!!!

--YOU, *LOOK* AT YOU! CAN'T *BELIEVE*--

...*DELA* DIDN'T THINK I'D MAKE THE CONNECTION...

SOMEONE'S *MEETING* US?

--THEN MY *BELT,* THEN MY *SHOES,* FOR GOD'S SAKE!

--NO IDEA HOW MUCH I MISSED YOU--

EXCUSE ME. I SAID, *EXCUSE* ME--

THAT'S WHAT STACY SAID.

THOSE *TWO.*

KEYSTONE *home of the:* FLASH

YEAH.

DETECTIVE CHYRE?

THAT'D BE ME. YOU'RE *ALLEN?*

CRISPUS ALLEN, YEAH...

...THIS IS MY *PARTNER,* RENEE MONTOYA.

JARED MORILLO.

NICE TO MEET YOU.

ALLEN. YOU'VE GOT A *GOOD* NAME FOR *THIS* TOWN, DETECTIVE.

HOW'S THAT?

USED TO BE ONE OF THE TECHNICAL GUYS BY THE *SAME* NAME, BARRY ALLEN.

HE WAS BLACK?

WHITE AS MICHAEL BOLTON.

HOPE YOU BOTH ARE WEARING YOUR *LONG JOHNS.* NO TELLING *WHEN* THIS STORM'S GOING TO END.

FORECAST THIS MORNING WAS FOR *CLEAR* AND *COLD.*

YEAH, THAT'S WHAT *WE'D* HEARD, TOO.

HOP IN, WE'LL HEAD STRAIGHT OUT TO *IRON HEIGHTS.*

WEATHER WIZARD'S *LOOSE,* COULD BE *HIM.*

CHYRE, TURN ON THE *HEATER.*

IT'S STILL *BUSTED.*

WEST SAID HE'D *FIX* IT.

GUESS HE DIDN'T HAVE THE *TIME.*

NO PARKIN OR STANDI

YOU HEARD FROM OUR **CAPTAIN**?

THE D.A.s ARE **TALKING.** I THINK IT'S A **BAD** IDEA, THOUGH, CUTTING A **DEAL** WITH HIM.

DESMOND'S ONE OF THE **SMARTEST** OF THE ROGUES. NUTS, BUT **BRILLIANT.**

"ROGUES"?

YEAH, THEY'RE A GROUP OF **METAs,** WORK TOGETHER TO MAKE **OUR** LIVES **MISERABLE.**

CHRIST, THEY'VE **UNIONIZED?**

YOUR GUYS DON'T DO THAT?

GUNS AND SHIELDS, KIDS.

OUR GUYS **RARELY** COOPERATE.

I WENT OVER SOME CASE **FILES. DESMOND** COULD'VE RUN TO GOTHAM ABOUT EIGHTEEN MONTHS BACK.

PROBABLY WHEN HE SET THAT LITTLE **BOOBY TRAP** YOUR OFFICER FOUND.

DOCTOR ZOLOMON IS WAITING FOR YOU INSIDE.

THANKS, GEOFF.

ALL RIGHT, WE'RE GOOD. IT'S **THIS** WAY--

GIMME A SECOND.

DOCTOR ZOLOMON.

HMM?

THESE ARE THE DETECTIVES FROM GOTHAM.

RIGHT. ASHLEY ZOLOMON, I'M THE ROGUE PROFILER FOR THE KEYSTONE P.D.

YOU HAVE YOUR *OWN* STAFF PROFILER?

WE SHOULD GET ONE OF THOSE.

DOCTOR DESMOND HAS BEEN MOVED INTO SECURE *HOLDING* SO YOU CAN SPEAK WITH HIM.

I'LL REMAIN OUT HERE WITH DETECTIVES MORILLO AND CHYRE.

ALPHA HOLDING

IN ADDITION TO THE *OBVIOUS* SAFETY PROTOCOLS, YOU SHOULD KNOW THE *FOLLOWING* THINGS BEFORE YOU SPEAK TO HIM.

HE'S *BRILLIANT* AND *MANIPULATIVE.* HE WILL TRY TO MANIPULATE *YOU.*

THE THING HE *CARES* FOR *MOST* IS HIS *WORK.* HE DOES *NOT* CONSIDER HIMSELF A *CRIMINAL,* BUT RATHER A *SCIENTIST.*

APPEAL TO HIM AS A *MAN OF SCIENCE,* DETECTIVES...

...BUT BE *CAREFUL* THAT *YOU'RE* THE ONES MANIPULATING *HIM...*

"...AND *NOT* THE OTHER WAY *AROUND*."

NEW *FACES*.

THIS *IS* EXCITING.

AND FROM *FAR* AWAY.

GOTHAM CITY.

SOMEONE FOUND THE *EXPERIMENT*, THAT'S *IT*, ISN'T IT? EMBRACED MY *FIRES OF CREATION* AND THUS ARE THEY *CHANGED*.

AND HERE YOU STAND, SEEKING MY *WISDOM*, HOPING TO *COMPREHEND* THAT WHICH IS *BEYOND* YOUR KEN.

YOU *CAN'T*. DON'T EVEN *TRY*.

BUT ASK *NICELY*, AND PERHAPS I'LL *HELP* YOU ALL THE SAME.

DOCTOR DESMOND, MY NAME'S DETECTIVE ALLEN. THIS IS MY *PARTNER* DETECTIVE MONTOYA.

THINK YOU CAN *ANSWER* A FEW *QUESTIONS* FOR US?

QUID PRO *QUO,* DETECTIVE ALLEN...

...OR FOR THOSE OF YOU *WEAK* WITH THE *LATIN,* "SOMETHING FOR SOMETHING."

TWO DETECTIVES COME *ALL* THE WAY FROM *GOTHAM* TO MINE MY *GRAY MATTER,* WHAT DO I GET IN *RETURN?*

DEPENDING ON YOUR *LEVEL* OF *COOPERATION,* THE *WARDEN* IS WILLING TO *OFFER* YOU CERTAIN *CONCESSIONS.*

ACCESS TO YOUR *RESEARCH,* FOR INSTANCE.

VERY GOOD, DETECTIVE ALLEN. NO *HINT* OF *HESITATION.*

BUT WE *BOTH* KNOW THAT YOU'RE *LYING* TO ME. WARDEN WOLFE WOULD NEVER ALLOW FOR SUCH AN *ARRANGEMENT.*

TRY *AGAIN.*

LET'S *HEAR* WHAT YOU'VE *GOT.*

THEN WE'LL DECIDE WHAT IT'S *WORTH* TO US.

²TSK TSK TSK²

DETECTIVE MONTOYA, *REALLY.* YOU KNOW HOW TO PLAY *BAD COP* BETTER THAN *THAT.*

IF YOU'RE **NOT** GOING TO BRING YOUR **BEST** GAME, I SEE NO **REASON** TO PLAY AT ALL.

SIT BACK DOWN.

OR WHAT? YOU'LL COME IN **HERE** AND BEAT ON ME? I **DOUBT** THAT.

I THINK I'LL ASK THE **SCREW** TO **RETURN** ME TO MY **CELL**.

DO THAT AND YOU **LOSE** YOUR CHANCE TO **PROVE** HOW MUCH **SMARTER** THAN US YOU **ARE**.

OH, **VERY** GOOD.

YOU'VE **KEPT** ME IN THE **ROOM**, WELL DONE. QUID PRO QUO, SOMETHING FOR SOMETHING.

BUT THAT **DOESN'T** BUY YOU **ANSWERS**.

THEN WHAT **DOES?**

YOU ASK **YOUR** QUESTIONS. THEN **I'LL** ASK **MINE**.

HONESTY **BREEDS** TRUST, DETECTIVES. BUT YOU LIE TO **ME**, AND I'LL **LIE** TO YOU.

AND I **WILL** KNOW IF YOU ARE **LYING**, BELIEVE ME.

YOU GO FIRST.

...AS OF SIX HOURS AGO, THE **MUTATION** SEEMS TO HAVE **STABILIZED.**

GOTHAM CITY, ST. LUKE'S HOSPITAL.

WHETHER THAT'S A **RESULT** OF MOVING OFFICER KELLY INTO THE **CLEAN ROOM** OR SOMETHING ELSE, WE CAN'T TELL.

HE'S STILL ON **DIAZEPAM?**

LOW DOSAGE THROUGH THE I.V. I DON'T WANT TO **RISK** ANOTHER **SEIZURE.**

AND STILL **NON-**RESPONSIVE?

...SINCE LAST NIGHT. EYES ARE **OPEN,** BUT **NOBODY'S** HOME.

WHO'RE **THEY?** FAMILY?

SHE'S KELLY'S **GIRLFRIEND.** THE OTHER ONE IS HIS **PARTNER.**

THEY'RE **NOT** GOING TO WANT TO **WATCH** THIS.

CLOSE THE **BLINDS,** PLEASE.

YES, DOCTOR.

HEY...SHARON, NO, IT'LL BE ALL RIGHT.

ANDY'S TOUGH, HE'LL PULL THROUGH.

I DON'T...

...I DON'T UNDERSTAND!

WHAT'S HAPPENING TO HIM?

WHY WOULD SOMEONE DO THIS?

WHY?

I DON'T KNOW, HONEY.

I DON'T KNOW.

KNOWLEDGE, OF COURSE.

WHAT IS THE PURPOSE OF **ANY** EXPERIMENT, AFTER ALL?

MY TURN, NOW.

IS OFFICER--KELLY, IS IT?--IS OFFICER KELLY **STILL** UNDERGOING THE **TRANSFORMATION**, OR HAS THE **PROCESS** ARRESTED ITSELF?

LAST WE **HEARD** FROM THE HOSPITAL, HE'D **STABILIZED**.

OUR TURN.

THIS **EXPERIMENT** OR **TRANSFORMATION** OR **WHATEVER** YOU WANT TO CALL IT...

CAN IT BE **UNDONE?** CAN **YOU** UNDO IT?

THAT'S **TWO** QUESTIONS, DETECTIVE. THE ANSWER TO **BOTH** IS YES.

HMM... LOOK AT **YOU**... FRESH **SCAR** TISSUE ON YOUR **KNUCKLES** AND AROUND YOUR EYE...

...YOU SEEM TO HAVE DEVELOPED A **TASTE**--IF NOT A **DELIGHT**--FOR **VIOLENCE** RECENTLY, DETECTIVE.

I ALSO NOTE THE **DOUBLE VENUS** PENDANT YOU'RE WEARING AT YOUR **THROAT**...

...**GAY PRIDE** IS SUCH A **WONDERFUL** THING...

JUST ASK YOUR DAMN QUESTION.

IT'S A **KNOWN** FACT THAT INCIDENCES OF **DOMESTIC VIOLENCE** IN SAME-SEX RELATIONSHIPS IS QUITE **HIGH**. IT'S **ALSO** QUITE HIGH AMONGST **POLICE OFFICERS**.

SO MY **QUESTION** IS **THIS**:

DO YOU **BEAT** HER, DETECTIVE DYKE?

YOU SON OF A BITCH.

IS THAT A YES?

QUID PRO QUO, REMEMBER. TELL THE TRUTH.

RENEE--

HE EXPECTS ME TO DIGNIFY THAT, TO ACTUALLY RESPOND TO THAT?

WE NEED HIS HELP.

STATISTICALLY, INCIDENCES OF DOMESTIC VIOLENCE ARE IDENTICAL FOR STRAIGHTS AND GAYS, DOCTOR DESMOND--

YOU'RE AVOIDING MY QUESTION.

DO YOU BEAT HER, DETECTIVE?

NEVER IN MY LIFE.

HOW DO WE CURE KELLY?

YOU DON'T.

I DO.

AND THE PENNY DROPS.

HOW?

THAT I CAN'T ANSWER, I'M AFRAID, NOT UNTIL I SEE THE EXPERIMENT.

...DISCUSS YOUR **ATTEMPTS** TO COMBAT THE ENDEMIC **RACISM** IN THE DEPARTMENT BY APPEARING TO BE **WHITE**, DETECTIVE ALLEN?

COULD WE TURN THE REPLAY **OFF**?

I **WARNED** YOU.

IT'S **NOTHING** WE HAVEN'T **SEEN** BEFORE.

NICE GOOD COP-BAD COP ROUTINE YOU GOT GOING THERE.

THANKS, **MORILLO**.

HE'S **PLAYING** US, HE'S GOING TO TELL US **ANYTHING** HE THINKS WE WANT TO **HEAR**.

AS LONG AS IT **REINFORCES** HIS **CONCEIT** THAT HE'S MORE **INTELLIGENT** THAN THE TWO OF YOU, YES.

THAT **DOESN'T** MEAN HE'S **LYING**, THOUGH. HE **COULD** KNOW HOW TO **SAVE** THIS **OFFICER** OF OURS.

YOU HEARD HIM YOURSELF, ALLEN. DESMOND DOESN'T **CARE** ABOUT YOUR **COP**.

FAR AS HE'S **CONCERNED**, THIS KELLY GUY IS AN **EXPERIMENT**, NOT A **PERSON**. HE'S GOT **NO** INTEREST IN **CURING** HIM AT **ALL**.

THEN FIGURE DESMOND **WANTS** TO SEE HIS **HANDIWORK**, RIGHT?

THAT'S WHAT HE'S **AFTER**, HE WANTS TO SEE WHAT HE'S DONE TO KELLY UP **CLOSE**.

SO YOU TAKE HIM TO **GOTHAM** AND HOPE DESMOND SEES YOUR GUY AND **SUFFERS** AN ATTACK OF **CONSCIENCE**?

YOU **CAN'T** BE **THAT** NAIVE.

I'M NOT SEEING ANY OTHER **OPTION**.

I DON'T KNOW, MAYBE DESMOND *SEES* KELLY, SOMETHING SHAKES *LOOSE.*

SOME- THING WE CAN *USE.*

IF WISHES WERE *HORSES.*

PROBABLY WHY THERE AREN'T ANY HORSES IN GOTHAM.

YOU'LL *EXCUSE* US, WE NEED TO MAKE A COUPLE OF *CALLS.*

THINK WE CAN GET THE *DEPARTMENT* TO SPRING FOR *TWO* TICKETS TO *GOTHAM?*

YOU WANT TO *BABYSIT* THIS *DISASTER-IN-THE- MAKING?*

THEY'RE GONNA GIVE THAT *LUNATIC* JUST WHAT HE *WANTS.*

THAT *DOESN'T* MEAN *THEY* WON'T GET WHAT *THEY* WANT IN *TURN,* DETECTIVE CHYRE.

ALBERT DESMOND IS--TO PUT IT *BLUNTLY*--AN *ARROGANT BASTARD.*

HE *LIKES* TO *GLOAT,* AND IF THEY GIVE HIM *ENOUGH* ROPE, THERE'S A CHANCE DOCTOR ALCHEMY COULD *MAKE HIS OWN NOOSE.*

MAYBE IT'LL BE A NOOSE, DOCTOR ZOLOMON...

...BUT I'M THINKING IT MIGHT BE *MORE* LIKE A *LEASH...*

...AND THAT *THIS* IS JUST ONE *WILD-GOOSE CHASE.*

ALPHA HOLDING

SIR? YOU HAVE A *MINUTE?*

WHAT CAN I *DO* FOR YOU, CAPTAIN SAWYER?

THAT'S MY *PROBLEM,* SIR.

I'M *NOT SURE* MYSELF.

ALL RIGHT, I'M *INTRIGUED.*

EXPLAIN, MAGGIE.

IT'S ABOUT THE *THING* WITH OFFICER KELLY.

ALLEN AND MONTOYA ARE OUT IN *KEYSTONE,* THEY'VE BEEN TALKING TO DOCTOR ALCHEMY. THEY WANT TO *BRING* HIM *HERE.*

ALCHEMY HAS ADMITTED THAT HE'S *RESPONSIBLE* FOR KELLY'S CONDITION?

YES, SIR, COMMISSIONER.

THING IS, ALCHEMY'S *ALSO* CLAIMING HE CAN *CURE* KELLY.

BUT HE NEEDS TO *SEE* THE...*PATIENT...* FIRST.

OF COURSE HE DOES.

MONTOYA AND ALLEN, THEY THINK HE'S ON THE *LEVEL?*

IF THERE IS A *CURE,* ALCHEMY KNOWS IT.

WHETHER HE'LL *DO* IT OR *NOT,* THAT'S SOMETHING *ELSE.*

YOU'VE SPOKEN TO THE KEYSTONE PEOPLE ABOUT TRANSFERRING DOCTOR ALCHEMY TO OUR *CUSTODY?*

I MADE SOME INITIAL *INQUIRIES,* BUT ULTIMATELY, IT HAS TO COME FROM *YOU* AND THE DISTRICT ATTORNEY.

WOULD WE BE TRYING THIS *HARD* TO SAVE KELLY IF HE *WASN'T* A COP, MAGGIE?

I DON'T KNOW.

BUT HE *IS* A COP, MIKE...

...AND ACCORDING TO *EVERYONE* WHO KNOWS HIM, A DAMN *GOOD* ONE.

AND THERE ARE *FEW* ENOUGH OF *THOSE* IN THIS CITY.

ALL RIGHT, I'LL CALL THEIR D.A.

THANK YOU, SIR.

...SO IT'S **APPROVED**, THEN?

NOK NOK NOK

...WHAT DO YOU MEAN, A **CONDITION?** WHAT DOES THAT MEAN, MORILLO?

...AND YOU GUYS **CLEARED** THAT WITH **OUR** PEOPLE ALREADY...?

...HUH...NO, DOESN'T **BUG** ME, WE'VE GOT **ENOUGH** FREAKS IN GOTHAM, WE DON'T NEED TO ADD **YOURS**, TOO...

...HEH, NO, THAT'S A **DIFFERENT** STORY...

ALL RIGHT, WE'LL SEE YOU AT THE **AIRPORT**.

DONE DEAL?

YEAH. MORILLO AND CHYRE WILL **ESCORT** ALCHEMY TO GOTHAM **WITH** US ON THE **RED-EYE** TONIGHT, TAKE HIM **BACK** AS SOON AS WE'RE **DONE**.

THAT WAY, KEYSTONE **MAINTAINS** CUSTODY, AS OPPOSED TO RENDERING HIM TO **US**.

GOOD FOR US, ROTTEN FOR **THEM**, ESPECIALLY IF **SOMETHING** HAPPENS.

TELL ME ABOUT IT.

HOLD ON...

...DAMMIT...

DEE? HEY, IT'S **ME**. GUESS YOU'RE STILL AT THE **RESTAURANT**...

...CRIS AND I ARE STILL IN **KEYSTONE**, WE'RE FLYING BACK LATE TONIGHT.

JUST WANTED TO SAY THAT I MISS YOU...

...AND I LOVE YOU.

KLIK

I BEG YOUR PARDON...

...I'M LOOKING FOR MY DAUGHTER, RENEE...

...I UNDERSTAND SHE LIVES...HERE...

...YOU...YOU MUST BE MS. HERNANDEZ?

DARIA HERNANDEZ.

RENEE'S NOT HERE RIGHT NOW, SHE'S OUT OF TOWN--

I SEE.

I...I WON'T TROUBLE YOU, THEN...

MISTER MONTOYA.

PERHAPS...

WOULD YOU LIKE TO COME INSIDE?

PERHAPS FOR A FEW MINUTES, THANK YOU.

YOU DON'T WANT TO PICK UP ANYTHING FOR DORE? OR YOUR KIDS?

MY **WIFE** AND **KIDS** DON'T NEED A **SHIRT** PROVING THAT I **SURVIVED** A **FLIGHT** TO KEYSTONE CITY.

THIS HASN'T BEEN A **TOURIST** TRIP, PARTNER.

YOU'RE **AFRAID** TO FLY. THAT'S **IT**, ISN'T IT?

SHUT UP.

HERE THEY **ARE**.

NOTHING **QUITE** AS DEPRESSING AS AN **AIRPORT** IN THE MIDDLE OF THE **NIGHT**, IS THERE?

THE **REEK** OF **MELANCHOLY** AND **DESPERATION**.

DETECTIVE **DYKE** AND DETECTIVE **STOWE**. HOW **NICE** TO **SEE** YOU BOTH AGAIN.

STOWE?

HARRIET BEECHER STOWE. WROTE **UNCLE TOM'S CABIN**.

SEE, HE'S CALLING ME AN UNCLE TOM.

REALLY, DETECTIVE **CHYRE**, IF YOU NEED THESE THINGS **EXPLAINED** TO YOU, YOU'RE NOT GOING TO GET VERY **FAR** IN YOUR **CHOSEN** PROFESSION.

LUCKILY, WE HAVE THE **ENTIRE** FLIGHT TO WORK ON YOUR **CONTINUING** EDUCATION.

FIRST PUBLISHED IN 1852, **UNCLE TOM'S CABIN, OR LIFE AMONG THE LOWLY**, IS CONSIDERED BY **MANY** TO BE ONE OF THE CAUSES THAT LED TO THE CIVIL WAR...

DOCTOR LING, DOCTOR LING TO THE O.R.

DOCTOR VILLEGAS, PLEASE DIAL EXTENSION 5530.

...HEY...

HEY!

HELLO?

IS SOMEONE HERE?

ARGHAE RSPERATRA

ANDY? GOD, ANDY, CAN YOU *HEAR* ME?

SHHHAARONNN?

THE KID...

...DID KID...GET OUUUTT...?

HE'S FINE, ANDY, YOU *SAVED* HIM. HE'S *FINE*, THEY'RE *BOTH* FINE.

OH, GOD, ANDY...

NOOO...

...DOONNN'T CRY...

THESE ARE A **TEMPERED** STEEL, **AREN'T** THEY?

NOTHING MORE THAN WORKED **CARBON** AND **IRON**.

YOU TALK AN **AWFUL** LOT, YOU KNOW THAT, DOCTOR?

IT HELPS TO PASS THE **TIME**.

CERTAINLY MADE THE **FLIGHT** SEEM TO GO BY **QUICKLY**.

FOR **YOU**, MAYBE.

OKAY, HE'S IN THE I.C.U., APPARENTLY THEY JUST **MOVED** HIM OUT OF A **STERILE** ROOM.

INDEED? **WHY** WOULD THEY DO **THAT**?

HE'S GETTING **BETTER**, NO THANKS TO **YOU**.

MOVE IT.

COME ON, WE'LL TAKE THE **ELEVATOR**...

...THE **SPECIALIST** FROM S.T.A.R. IS **WAITING** FOR US IN THE I.C.U...

THAT WAS ROUGHLY **ONE** THIS MORNING.

HE'S BEEN **DRIFTING** IN AND OUT OF CONSCIOUSNESS EVER SINCE, BUT FOR THE TIME BEING, I'D SAY THAT OFFICER KELLY IS **STABLE**.

THEN YOU'RE AN **IDIOT**.

I BEG YOUR **PARDON?**

MONKEY WANT A 'NANA?

YOU'RE AN **IDIOT**, AN **IMBECILE**, A **MORON**.

WHAT DO YOU HAVE HIM ON? STEROIDS?

IT SEEMED THE **BEST** WAY TO BOLSTER--

YEAH, **IDIOT**, IT'S **NOT** HELPING HIM, IT'S **MASKING** THE **SYMPTOMS**, ALL RIGHT?

AND WHEN HE **DECOMPENSATES**-- AND HE **WILL**, SWEET CHEEKS--HE'LL **DIE**, DO YOU UNDERSTAND?

I'LL USE **SMALL** WORDS:

YOU. ARE. KILLING. HIM.

YOU'RE THE **LUNATIC** WHO **DID** THIS TO HIM?

GUILTY AS CHARGED.

THEN WHY IN THE **WORLD** WOULD I **BELIEVE** YOU CARE ABOUT **CURING** HIM?

MY **EXPERIMENT** WAS TO **CHANGE** HIM, **NOT** MURDER HIM.

AND YOU, YOU'RE **MURDERING** HIM, **NOT** CURING HIM.

LOOK, WE **BROUGHT** HIM ALL THIS **WAY** TO TAKE A **LOOK** AT HIM--

I'M **NOT** LETTING THIS **SOCIOPATH** NEAR MY **PATIENT**--

SCIENTIST! I'M A **SCIENTIST**--

--YOU BUBBLE-CHESTED **BIMBO** IN A LAB **COAT!**

EEEE EEEEE

EEEE EEEEEEEEE NURSE!

PADDLES!

OH NO, NO, NO--

--GOD NO PLEASE **PLEASE** NO--

HE'S **READY**.

AS AM I.

YOU KNOW THE *LEGEND* OF THE *PHILOSOPHER'S STONE*, DETECTIVES?

TRANSMUTING LEAD INTO *GOLD*?

CARBON AND *IRON* INTO HYDROGEN AND OXYGEN?

OR PERHAPS THE *STERLING SILVER* OF A SPECIAL *NECKLACE*--

SON OF A--

¡GHFF!

--INTO *HYDROGEN* AND *CHLORINE*?

HKHKKRRRRK

Keystone Kops Part Three

CERTIFICATE OF
APPRECIATION

Detective Crispus Allen in recognition of
Outstanding Achievement in Community Safety

GOTHAM CITY
POLICE DEPARTMENT

DATE
WITNE
RECOR

ALLEN/CRISPUSMR
KEYSTONE CITY
GOTHAM CITY
EAGLE AIRWAYS
US 306 V OGDRN 030R
A22 715A 28D NO

EAGLE AIRWAYS
ALLEN/CRISPUSMR
GOTHAM CITY
KEYSTONE CITY
EAGLE AIRWAYS
B32 1215P 9G NO

G. DESCRIPTION, SCARS, MARKS, M.O., ETC.

interview ALBERT DESMOND, a.k.a. DOCTOR ALCHEMY at Iron Heights Penitentiary
in Keystone City, in connection with Officer Andrew Kelly's worsening
condition. During the course of the interview between Desmond, Detective
Montoya and myself, it was determined that Desmond held the only possible
course of recovery for Officer Kelly's deteriorating condition.

After negotiation with the Keystone Prison Authority and District Attorney's
Office, conditional permission for the transport of Desmond from Keystone to
Gotham was obtained, with K.P.D. Detective Jared Morillo and Detective
Fred Chyre maintaining custody during transport.

Upon arriving at the hospital, Desmond managed to conjure or otherwise obtain
the artifact known as the Philosopher's Stone, which he then used to attemp
an escape.

Keystone Kops Part Four

ANDY, MY GOD--

...THOUGH IT SEEMS THAT YOURS IS JUST *BEGINNING.*

DETECTIVE, *STOP!*

HNNRR?

NHRH HNN HNN?

HNFF SNFHH.

FRSHHARRONN SNFF HN HNRRR HNRR--

ARRAARRRRR

YOU'RE IN THE **WRONG** TOWN, DOC.

I'VE **NEVER** HIT MY **GIRL**--

GHUH

--BUT I'LL **SURE** AS HELL BEAT **YOUR** ASS, MOTHER$#%* !

HKKK

...ALL UNITS, BUT THERE'S BEEN *NOTHING* FOR OVER AN *HOUR*.

SUN'S COMING *UP*, SO IT SHOULD MAKE THE *HUNT* EASIER.

NO CHANCE BATMAN CAUGHT UP WITH HIM?

IF HE *HAD*, WE'D HAVE *HEARD* ABOUT IT BY NOW.

YOU USE THAT *SIGNAL* THING OF YOURS?

NOT *ANYMORE*, WE *DON'T*.

MUST *SUCK* NOT TO BE ABLE TO *TRUST* YOUR *GUY*.

TELL ME ABOUT IT.

HOW'S THE **OTHER** ONE, THE **SPECIALIST?**

DOCTOR NICHOLS? DESMOND TURNED THE **AIR** IN HER **LUNGS** TO **PURE** OXYGEN, IT'S WHY SHE WENT **DOWN.**

SHE'S **RECOVERING.**

WHAT NOW, CAP?

UNTIL WE **FIND** KELLY, NOT A LOT WE **CAN** DO.

YOU TWO SHOULD GET OUT OF **HERE,** GET CLEANED UP, GET SOME **REST...**

...I'LL CALL IF ANYTHING **DEVELOPS.**

WHAT ABOUT US, CAPTAIN SAWYER?

WELL, MORILLO, WE'RE GONNA HAVE TO **HOLD** ONTO **DESMOND** FOR A FEW DAYS, AT LEAST TO **CHARGE** HIM.

YOU MEAN **AFTER** HE GETS OUT OF THE E.R.

LOOK, WE'RE **HERE,** CAPTAIN, WE'RE WILLING TO **HELP...**

HEY, MONTOYA...

YEAH, CHYRE?

THAT **MAKEOVER** YOU GAVE DOCTOR ALCHEMY.

YEAH?

NICELY DONE.

:KAFF:
:KOFF:

:KOFF:
:KAFF:

HEY.

HOW LONG YOU BEEN BACK?

NOT LONG.

:KAFF:

DIDN'T WANT TO WAKE YOU, SORRY--

OH MY GOD, RENEE--

--WHAT *HAPPENED,* DID YOU GET *BURNED?*

WHAT?

YOUR *SKIN...*

...LOOKS LIKE YOU GOT *BURNED...*

DOCTOR ALCHEMY SOUNDS POSITIVELY VILE.

YEAH, WELL, THAT'S WHY THEY CALL PEOPLE LIKE DESMOND SUPERVILLAINS, DEE.

AND YOU'RE OKAY? YOU FEEL ALL RIGHT?

THE COUGH FINALLY SEEMS TO HAVE GONE AWAY.

I'M JUST TIRED.

I'LL HAVE TO GET YOU A NEW NECKLACE.

DON'T YOU THINK IT'LL BE KIND OF REDUNDANT?

RENEE.

I'M JUST SAYING.

YOUR FATHER STOPPED BY WHILE YOU WERE IN KEYSTONE.

WHAT'D HE WANT?

TO SEE YOU.

HE MISSES YOU, RENEE...

...HE WANTS YOU BACK IN HIS LIFE.

MORNING, HERNANDO!

MORNING, VICTOR!

HAVE A GOOD DAY!

YOU, TOO.

...COMPARED KELLY'S BLOOD BEFORE **AND** AFTER ALCHEMY **ZAPPED** HIM.

AS FAR AS WE CAN TELL, DOCTOR ALCHEMY DIDN'T ACTUALLY **ADD** ANYTHING, ALL HE DID WAS **INCREASE** THE POTENCY OF THE **TOXIN** ALREADY IN KELLY'S **BODY.**

NOW THAT WE'VE **ISOLATED** IT, WE CAN WORK ON A **CURE.**

SO YOU'RE SAYING KELLY'S CONDITION **ISN'T** PERMANENT?

NOT **YET,** NO. IF WE CAN FIND HIM IN THE NEXT **TWELVE** HOURS, I BELIEVE WE **CAN** CURE HIM.

WE'RE TALKING ABOUT KELLY?

DOCTOR NICHOLS THINKS THERE'S A WAY TO CHANGE HIM BACK--

:KAFF KOFFKOFF:

WHAT DO YOU **NEED** FROM US?

PARDON ME.

YOU NEED TO **FIND** KELLY, **SUBDUE** HIM SOMEHOW.

THE **SOONER** I CAN ATTEND TO HIM, THE **BETTER** HIS CHANCES **ARE.**

WE HAVE **ANY** IDEA WHERE HE **IS?**

NOTHING AT ALL.

DESMOND **MIGHT** KNOW.

I'M **NOT** SAYING WE GIVE DESMOND A **SECOND** CHANCE TO **SCREW** US, I'M SAYING WE **TALK** TO HIM.

WHAT, SO HE CAN PLAY **MORE** OF HIS **HEAD** GAMES?

YOU GOT A **BETTER** IDEA, I'M **LISTENING**, FRED.

DESMOND STILL AT THE **HOSPITAL?**

HE WAS MOVED TO THE **SCHRECK** THREE HOURS AGO, UNDER **MAXIMUM** SECURITY.

WE'LL KEEP YOU **POSTED**, CAPTAIN.

⟨KOFF KOFF KOFF KOFF⟩

YOU DO THAT.

DING DING

OFFICER PEAK? I DIDN'T **RECOGNIZE** YOU OUT OF YOUR **UNIFORM**.

HEY, HERNANDO.

YEAH, I'M, UH... I'M TAKING THE **DAY**...

...OFF...

YOU DON'T LOOK SO GOOD, OFFICER.

ANDY'S ON THE **LOOSE**, I DON'T KNOW IF YOU **HEARD** IT ON THE **NEWS**.

TURNED INTO A **MONSTER** OR SOMETHING, HE'S...

...HE...HE **KILLED** HIS **GIRLFRIEND**, SHARON, HERNANDO...

...AT THE **HOSPITAL**, HE WAS OUT OF **CONTROL** AND HE...HE...

...I KEPT **TELLING** HER IT WOULD BE **OKAY**...

...I TOLD HER EVERYTHING WOULD BE **OKAY**...

YOU'LL GET **NO** HELP FROM **ME**.

IN FACT, THE **ONLY** THING YOU'LL BE GETTING FROM ME IS A **MASSIVE** SUIT FOR **DAMAGES**, FILED AGAINST DETECTIVE DYKE FOR **BRUTALITY**.

YOU WERE **RESISTING** ARREST.

SPTT

DAMNIT--

RENEE!

--GET **OFF** OF **ME**!

UH-OH, LOOK OUT--

--ANGRY LESBIAN, COMING **THROUGH**!

I'LL BE **OUTSIDE**.

NO, DON'T **LEAVE**...

...YOUR **BUTTONS** ARE SO **EASY** TO **PRESS**!

I MEAN IT, DETECTIVE! YOUR **SUBCONSCIOUS** IS SO **CLOSE** TO THE **SURFACE** I CAN SEE ITS **PERISCOPE**!

SHUT UP, ALBERT.

214

...DOWN TO THE *BUS* TO TAKE 'EM ALL TO *COURT* FOR THE *TEN* A.M...

--*MONSTER,* I'M TELLING YOU HE'S LIKE A GREEN HULKING *MONSTER*--

--*DIDN'T DO* ANYTHING I *SWEAR* TO *GOD!!!*

...FOLLOW THE RED LINE *PAINTED* ON THE FLOOR, TURN *LEFT*...

--*JUST* WANTED HIM TO PAY *ME* WHAT HE *OWED*--

--I DON'T *DO* FREEBIES, *THAT'S* WHY I *CUT* HIM--

HEY, *MONTOYA!*

OFFICER DOGNAVICH.

HEARD YOU GOT THE *S.O.B.* WHO *DID* KELLY.

HEARD YOU *WORKED* HIM OVER PRETTY *GOOD.*

GOOD *JOB.*

WHAT'S *YOUR* PROBLEM?

HNNKIDDZZ

SSVVVTHHKIDDZZZ

SKRRE

HNKK
HNKK

...RESOLVED, TEN-FIFTY. BACK IN SERVICE. ⦃SKSS⦄

⦃SKCHH⦄ ANGEL FOUR-ELEVEN, TEN-FOUR. ⦃SKCHH⦄

⦃SKSS⦄ ALL UNITS, TEN-THIRTY-THREE IN PROGRESS...

...META-HUMAN DISTURBANCE, FIRE AND E.M.S. EN ROUTE...

...KELLY...

...FIFTEEN HUNDRED BLOCK AT VAN BUREN...

OH MY GOD--

RENEE? RENEE, WAIT! WHERE THE HELL--

--OH MY GOD, PAPI--

--ARE YOU GOING...?

218

THE END

GREG RUCKA is the author of several novels, including *Finder, Keeper, Smoker, Shooting at Midnight, Critical Space,* and *Patriot Acts* (all of which feature the bodyguard character Atticus Kodiak), plus *Private Wars* and *A Gentleman's Game* (featuring the *Queen & Country* character Tara Chace), *A Fistful of Rain* and more.

In comics, he has written some of the most well known characters in the world, on titles such as BATMAN, WONDER WOMAN, *Wolverine,* and *Elektra.* Other work includes titles such as 52 (with Geoff Johns, Grant Morrison and Mark Waid), GOTHAM CENTRAL and *Daredevil* (with Ed Brubaker), CHECKMATE, and FINAL CRISIS: REVELATIONS. Currently he is writing DC's longest-running titles, ACTION COMICS and DETECTIVE COMICS.

His creator-owned comics include the award-winning *Queen & Country* and *Whiteout* (which is now a major motion picture starring Kate Beckinsale).

ED BRUBAKER is a one-time cartoonist whose early work in comics includes *Pajama Chronicles, Purgatory USA,* and *Lowlife.* He soon began predominantly writing comics, garnering attention for stories such as the Eisner Award-nominated "An Accidental Death," *The Fall,* and SCENE OF THE CRIME.

Brubaker began alternating his writing projects between DC's mainstream comics line, their mature-readers imprint Vertigo, and their WildStorm imprint. Some projects included BATMAN, DEADENDERS, SANDMAN PRESENTS: DEAD BOY DETECTIVES, CATWOMAN, SLEEPER, THE AUTHORITY, and GOTHAM CENTRAL (with Greg Rucka).

Currently, he is writing for Marvel Comics, including *Daredevil* and *Captain America* for their superhero line, and *Criminal* and *Incognito* for their Icon imprint.

MICHAEL LARK has been drawing his whole life, but his first published mainstream comics work was in 1994 — illustrating the Dean Motter-written TERMINAL CITY for Vertigo.

Since then, Lark's unique film noir style has been showcased in SCENE OF THE CRIME, LEGEND OF THE HAWKMAN, TERMINAL CITY: AERIAL GRAFFITI, SANDMAN MYSTERY THEATRE, SUPERMAN: WAR OF THE WORLDS, BATMAN: NINE LIVES, GOTHAM CENTRAL, *The Pulse,* and *Captain America.* Lark also has the honor of illustrating bestselling author Michael Chabon's first comics work, featured in JSA ALL STARS.

Currently, Lark is the artist on Marvel's *Daredevil* series, written by his GOTHAM CENTRAL comrade Ed Brubaker.

STEFANO GAUDIANO was born in Milan, Italy, and moved to the U.S. in the early '80s. Soon after, Gaudiano became a comic book artist and published the Eisner Award-nominated limited series *Kafka* (with Steven T. Seagle) while still in college. His art has since been featured in *Dark Horse Presents,* SANDMAN MYSTERY THEATRE, CATWOMAN, BATMAN: FAMILY, *Daredevil, The Pulse, Captain Marvel,* and many more books.

Gaudiano has also done art for other media, including storyboards for the likes of *Spider-Man Unlimited* and *Monster Mash,* as well as illustrations for roleplaying games like *HeroQuest.*